IMMERSED
in the Passion

Oberammergau's Unique Experience
Shared with the World

Peter Walker

Walkway Books UK

Published by:

Walkway
B O O K S

All permission and other requests may be handled through our publisher website:
walkwaybooks.com

ISBN 978-1-9163689-0-3

Acknowledgments:

Scriptures taken from the Holy Bible, New International Version®, NIV®. Copyright © 1973, 1978, 1984, 2011 by Biblica, Inc.™ Used by permission of Zondervan. All rights reserved worldwide. www.zondervan.com The "NIV" and "New International Version" are trademarks registered in the United States Patent and Trademark Office by Biblica, Inc.™

Unless otherwise noted, all photographs are courtesy of Dr Peter Walker and Educational Opportunities.

Cover photo of Garden Tomb is courtesy of flickr.com/upyernoz.

Special thanks to Mark Yeh (Educational Opportunities), Rob Wendover (Prologue Sales), and Jacqui Crawford Design.

Image of Oberammergau pastoral team on pages 8, 30 (Father Gröner), and back cover are courtesy of Stephan Fenzl/SF Online Oberammergau. http://fenzl-web.de/

Map on page 5 courtesy of Peter Hermes Furian/Shutterstock.com.

Cast and crew photos on pages 25, 28, 34, 37, and 44 are copyright ©Passion Play Oberammergau 2020/Gabriela Neeb.

Photos on pages 36, 60, 65, 68, 81, and 92 are copyright ©Passion Play Oberammergau 2020.

Map on page 48 courtesy of Leandro PP/Shutterstock.com.

Image on page 76 courtesy of Flik47/Shutterstock.com.

Image on page 105 courtesy of Mordechai Meiri/Shutterstock.com.

Illustration on page 107 courtesy of Olesssia/Shutterstock.com

Author photos on page 110 are courtesy of Graham Naylor (Ridley Hall, Cambridge).

Book cover and interior design by Tim Cobb.

CONTENTS

Alistair McCabe

James Ridgway

INTRODUCTION

For both our travel companies the task of taking thousands of passengers to experience the Passion Play in Oberammergau has been one of the greatest joys and privileges within our professional experience. Educational Opportunities (based in the USA) first brought visitors to the village in 1970 and McCabe Pilgrimages (based in the UK) in 1990. Every ten years since then, our companies have had to rise to the challenge—adding extra staff, setting up our programmes some three years beforehand, and juggling the uncertainties of exchange rates long in advance—but it has always been so worthwhile! Many people come back to us, saying that attending the Passion Play was one of the high points of their lives. Our hope is that the same will be true for many during this coming season in 2020.

A key part in our role is to collaborate with the Oberammergau authorities. For a small village to lay on such a production five times a week—as well as to give overnight hospitality to a good number of the 4,500 people in the audience for each performance—is a huge undertaking. It requires many years of planning and logistics. It also requires trust—with travel companies working cooperatively within the system devised by the village and keeping their promises. Our experience has been that there is no substitute for us coming to meet the organizing team several years in advance and then working closely with them as the season approaches. We enjoyed meeting Walter Rutz, Frederik Mayet, and their very able team and want to thank them here for all that they have been doing to prepare to welcome people from all over the world during these next few months.

We are looking forward to the 2020 season! We are particularly pleased to have commissioned this unique resource from Dr Peter Walker. Peter has written several books on biblical topics (including the popular illustrated guidebooks *In the Steps of Jesus* and *In the Steps of Paul*), and we've enjoyed having him lead tours for both our companies over the years—both in the Holy Land and around the Mediterranean. He has also led two groups to Oberammergau (for McCabe Pilgrimages) in 2000 and in 2010. We cannot think of a better qualified person to produce this book.

During August 2019, Peter stayed in Oberammergau and met the people whose reflections you can read here. For many of these meetings, he was accompanied by Werner Bischof (McCabe's local partner for the Oberammergau seasons since 2000), who was able to translate for Peter. People in the village were very gracious in the gift of their time. For example, Peter was able to chat with the director, Christian Stückl, for over five hours. Werner was impressed with how open people were to talking in this way. Warm and friendly conversations developed in which people shared things that were very important to them. The result is that these reflections will give you a unique opportunity to hear directly from people you may see but never actually meet—the villagers, the production team, and the actors on stage—and hear something of their own personal commitment to the Passion Play.

We hope these reflections—together with all the other background information and insights given by Peter as a biblical scholar—will really add to your experience of the Passion Play. Some may want to read this through before they attend the Play. Others may use it afterwards to give their experiences even more depth. Either way, we hope *Immersed in the Passion* will help you experience the Play and your visit to the village in a whole new way. Oberammergau's Passion Play is indeed a "unique experience" to be "shared with the world."

James Ridgway and Alistair McCabe

Pfarrer
Peter Sachi

Father
Thomas Gröner

Doctor
Angelika Winterer

Before, during, and after the Passion Play

A WARM WELCOME
awaits you from the
village of Oberammergau

To experience the Passion Play and to be immersed in the story of Jesus' life and death for more than five hours in a day is for many of you in the audience a unique experience in your lives—sometimes even overwhelming. New thoughts come to your minds, your emotions can be stirred, and you may need some time to think through and to process all that you have thought and felt.

That's why we in the village's Catholic and the Lutheran parishes, working together as an ecumenical team, have created other opportunities each day during the Passion Play season so that you can continue with your own thoughts and reflections. In the centre of the village, for example, there is an open space in the so-called *Sternplatz* ("Place of the Star"), which highlights themes such as trust, fear, and resurrection—all designed to help you to make connections between the story of the Passion and your own life.

Moreover, on each performance day (Sunday, Tuesday, Thursday, Friday, and Saturday) the following programme is offered within the village's churches:

- In the Catholic church of St. Peter and Paul, located on Ettaler Straße, masses are held each day in English at 8:00 a.m.; there is also a twenty-minute "light and text" installation playing continuously each evening from 9:00 p.m.
- In the Lutheran Kreuzkirche ('Church of the Cross'), located one hundred yards to the east of the theatre, communion services are held at 9:30 a.m. (on Sundays at 10:00 a.m.); there is also an organ recital and short prayer service before the start of the Play and an 'Open House' during the Interval.

In all of these places you will find people from the village who are willing to talk with you—only if you wish—and wanting to assist you in any way that might be helpful. We hope you will experience not just open doors but open hearts to welcome you. For we truly want you to have a full "Oberammergau experience'—not just seeing the Passion Play but allowing it to have its full effect upon you. Please enjoy being in our village, drink in its atmosphere, and experience our Bavarian hospitality!

We read in the Gospels of the welcome Jesus himself gave to the crowds:

> *When Jesus saw a large crowd, he had compassion on them,*
> *because they were like sheep without a shepherd. So he began*
> *to teach them many things (Mark 6:34).*

As people entrusted with pastoral care within the local church community, we are aware of our privilege in being available to come alongside people—from all over the world who have a wide variety of backgrounds and beliefs—and in being able to listen in an open-hearted way to whatever our visitors are sharing. Compassion means literally to "suffer alongside someone" or to "go through an experience together." That's what we are seeking to do in Oberammergau—coming alongside you as our visitors to experience the Passion together.

There is also a sense in which coming to Oberammergau turns out for many to be similar to going on a pilgrimage. Whatever their original motivation, people find it becomes in some way a journey of faith, helping them move forward through their lives with a new sense of direction, a clearer purpose, and a deeper understanding. For some, it can be expressly a time for discovering or rediscovering what it can mean to walk along the way of Jesus, to live one's life "the Jesus way."

Our motto as an ecumenical team ["Leidenschaft Lebe"] is based on the words for "passion" and "life." We even use a special red color to illustrate the words. In English, as in German, there are some double meanings in the word *passion*. One can speak of someone having a "life passion;" one can speak of someone experiencing a "passionate life" or "living a life of compassion." There are different shades of meaning. Our hope and prayer is that your visit to Oberammergau, as you give a day of your lives to being "immersed in the Passion," will indeed help you to return to your homes with a new vision for living out the story of Jesus and for being recognized as people who have been marked by your experience of his Passion.

Pfarrer Peter Sachi (pastor of the Lutheran church:
Evangelisch-Lutherische Kirchengemeinde)

Father Thomas Gröner (parish priest) and
Dr Angelika Winterer (pastoral coworker in the Catholic
parish church: Katholische Pfarrgemeinde Oberammergau)

If you or your group would like to be in touch with us during your visit to Oberammergau, our contact details can be found on the website: http://oberammergau-evangelisch.de/passion-play-2020/. The website for the Catholic church is http://www.pfarrverband-oberammergau.de/passionsseite/.

Herzlich willkommen!

PART I
Setting the Scene

THE PASSION IN JERUSALEM

Its Centrality within the Biblical Story

Introduction

A "drop in the ocean"? Is that what we are dealing with when we turn to consider the story of Jesus of Nazareth and his death in Jerusalem—something small and insignificant? Or is it more like a large boulder, dropped from a great height, pounding into the streets below—something powerful in its impact and long-lasting in its repercussions? When something is dropped, we soon realize, its overall effect is a combination both of what is dropped (its identity) and where it is dropped (its location).

Arguably—given that we are still talking about it 2000 years later—the Passion Story, which traces the events leading up to Jesus' crucifixion, has had an effect quite disproportionate to what one might have expected: why on earth are we still talking about the death of a Jewish teacher so many years after all of his contemporaries are long since "dead and gone"? It has evidently had a wide-ranging and long-term impact.

Is that because the other characters in the story are so interesting or that they are acting in ways so completely different to normal? No. It's because of who Jesus himself was (his identity) and where precisely this dramatic story was being acted out (his location).

For it turns out that Jerusalem was no ordinary place; instead it was a city at the centre of an ancient story, going back millennia, which was full of promise and which made claims to be the true story at the centre of the whole world. Jesus was no ordinary character. Instead, he was a person who, endorsed by his fine teaching and apparent acts of incredible power, was claiming to be the long-awaited central character in that ancient story contained in the Bible. It was this combination—the arrival of this Jesus in this Jerusalem—that caused the "sparks to fly." The coming of Jesus was like a great and mighty stone being dropped from a vast height, and his coming to Jerusalem meant the stone was about to land at a key centre in the ancient world. No wonder we are still feeling the "ripple-effect."

That's one reason—amongst many others—why a small Bavarian village is still performing its world-famous Passion Play in a "performance season" that has lasted nearly four hundred years. This feat is quite an incredible achievement on the part of this small village! And, although at one level a play performed by rural villagers might seem to be fairly insignificant—just a "drop in the ocean"—at another level we can begin to see how it is also an extraordinary phenomenon with an impact disproportionate to its actual size. Oberammergau's Passion Play indeed offers a "unique experience shared with the world." When asking why this is so, one might conclude that it is because the story it is seeking to retell turns out indeed to be the story at the epicentre of the entire world.

* * * * * *

As we delve into this unique phenomenon—the dramatic reenactment in a small village of a story from ancient Jerusalem—we will go back in the first three chapters to look at each of these three elements:

- in "The Passion in Jerusalem," the story's historical background in Jerusalem (as seen in the Gospels) and its original impact in the first-century world;
- in "The Passion in Oberammergau," the history of the Play within the life of Oberammergau through the last four hundred years;
- and in "The Passion on Stage," the challenges of enacting this story in dramatic form on stage within our modern world.

The Background to the Story

Jerusalem at the time of Jesus was a city with around twenty thousand inhabitants. At an elevation of nearly three thousand feet and located on a

View of Jerusalem from the Mount of Olives

line of hills, which formed a central spine down the length of the country from Samaria in the north to Hebron in the south, it was a city to which all visitors had to go "up"—whether from the Mediterranean coastal plain to the west or from the Jordan Valley and the Dead Sea to the east.

Founded by Israel's most famous king, David, and centred on the magnificent temple first built by his son, Solomon, Jerusalem had been at the centre of Israel's life for just over a thousand years—through the turbulent centuries of the kingdom ruled by David's heirs, through the dark days of Babylonian captivity and exile, through the era of the temple's restoration, and some years of joyful independence—but the city was now under enemy occupation. Jerusalem had shrunk to a shadow of its former self—now seemingly a small, insignificant place on the remote eastern borders of a vast and brutal empire.

So much history, so much hope, but now so much pain.

According to the Hebrew Scriptures (more often referred to as the Old Testament), Jerusalem was to be the setting for three annual religious festivals, one of which (Passover) celebrated the dramatic emancipation of the Hebrew slaves back in the days of Moses from under the yoke of Egypt's powerful ruler, the pharaoh. Not surprisingly, when Jerusalem's streets were crowded with Passover pilgrims (sometimes numbering 150,000, according to the Jewish historian Josephus), tensions could run high. The pilgrims longed for a new Moses, a new David, a new restorer of the temple, a new king—any or all of the above—if only they would somehow get rid of the hated Romans!

So much religious longing, so much ardent praying, and so much political tension. Jerusalem was like an oil tanker cruising dangerously on a seething wave of volcanic lava: it would only take one small spark and the whole thing would go up in flames.

It was into this prime location—this well-primed pressure-cooker, if you like—that Jesus calmly walked, advancing his own purposes, and announcing his surprising identity. Others were beginning to wonder if he was indeed the "Messiah"—the Hebrew term for the "anointed" king whom the people hoped would re-establish David's independent kingdom. What if they were right?

The Passion story is the story of what happened when the dynamic energy of Jesus' unique character encountered the pent-up frustrations and longings that were built into the very fabric of Jerusalem. It's a story about *his identity* in *this location*. That's the combination which gives the story its power.

The Impact of the Story

Imagine now that you and I tried explaining this background to some visitors from Mars. They might well conclude: "so Jesus, if he was indeed the Davidic King, presumably stormed into Jerusalem and routed the Romans! Have we got that right?"

Imagine their puzzled expressions when we reply, "No. Within a week Jesus was dead—put to death as a political agitator by those brutish Romans."

Most likely they would immediately reply: "So, very obviously, he was *not* the King. End of story! We can't work out why you're still talking about this dead-end story two thousand years later. There's no story here worth telling!"

Our Martian visitors' logic is compelling. But we have not told them the whole story. The writers of the four Gospels—the original sources for the story of Jesus—all affirm that the story did not end with Jesus' death. Something happened a few days later, which "flipped" the whole story—transforming it from a tale of tragedy into a journey of joy. In musical terms, the composer's score had suddenly shifted from a minor key to the major. Hope had been vindicated. "There was a sudden and unexpected twist in the story-line," we have to tell our Martian visitors. "And that's why we're still talking about it so many years later."

The impact of the Jesus-story depends—more perhaps than we often realize—on the story of the Resurrection, the claim made for his being raised physically from the dead. Without that ingredient in the story, there is simply no reason why anyone—whether in first-century Jerusalem, seventeenth-century Oberammergau, or the contemporary world—would still be talking about this story. Indeed, we might never even have heard the name of "Jesus of Nazareth." For why tell a story about a rural villager going up to a big city with some grandiose ideas but who gets crushed by the system?

The Gospel writers (Matthew, Mark, Luke, and John), even though they tell the story with slightly different colours and from different angles and perspectives, were all united in their answer: this story must be told because it was not just a true story about awful things that happened to good people. It was also a true story about what the God of Israel did through this Jesus amongst his own people—fully in keeping with their long-cherished hopes but also exceeding and transforming those hopes in many ways.

Moreover, they had to tell this story because, though it was a Jewish story, it was so much more than that. Jesus walked, as it were, into the story line of Israel, moved the plot forward, and then—through the dramatic "sting in the tail" of his Resurrection—blew the story wide open so that it now at last could go out to the wider world. Jesus "came to his own people," wrote John at the start of his Gospel. Yet, Jesus was also "coming into the world" in order to "give light" to a world shrouded in darkness. John wrote in the hope that his readers—wherever they may be in the world—would come to see that what this Jesus did in Jerusalem was indeed done for them and could transform their own worlds from darkness to light and from tragedy to joy.

This was the story's impact as it was felt in the first century. That's why the story has been told repeatedly ever since—through the eras of the Roman and Byzantine empires, through the so-called "Dark Ages" and the Medieval period, through the last four hundred years in Oberammergau, and now all around the globe.

The Passion story of Jesus was a true story. We might reasonably conclude that it took place in what seemed to be an unimportant city in the ancient world, but that city turned out to be the nerve-centre of the entire world. For it was the climactic story within an age-long larger story, contained within the Hebrew Scriptures, which was set up to bring blessing to all nations from one small people-group and to send out a message of good news from Jerusalem to the ends of the earth. The Jesus-story was the hinge on which the whole plot turned. So, the Passion story turns out to have been played out at the epicentre of divine purposes and, more truly, on a world-stage set against a universal backdrop. For it was—and indeed still is—a story *of* the world and *for* the world. It is thus the story, as many claim, that lies at the very centre of all human history.

THE PASSION IN OBERAMMERGAU
Its History within the Village

"There's no place like home!" Sometimes the desire to return to the place of one's upbringing and to be with one's own family is irresistible. So it must have felt for a young man called Kaspar Schisler, who for several months had been working on a farm in a Bavarian village called Eschenlohe, about ten miles from Oberammergau.

The year was 1632. The horrendous Thirty Years War, which would take the lives of millions of people, had been ravaging across Europe for the last ten years and bringing in its wake a deadly pestilence—almost certainly the bubonic plague. Oberammergau's sheltered location, surrounded by so many hills, had enabled the village to be spared thus far, but special precautionary measures had been taken: all people entering the valley were to be debarred entry or placed in quarantine. The plague was kept at bay until Kaspar, longing to be at home for Easter, sneaked in by night.

A few days later, he would be dead, his family infected; and, in due course, as can still be seen from the Parish Register of Deaths (the *Pestmatrikel*), some eighty or more villagers would lose their lives. In this dire situation, the leaders of the village came together in the church: "the village councils met," so the local chronicle attests, "and vowed to perform the Passion Play every ten years; and from this time on not a single person more died." Standing in front of the crucifix (which still stands on the right-hand side in the Catholic parish church), they made this solemn vow, which has been fulfilled to this day.

Such a vow might to us seem odd. Did they really think that such an act of penitence might avert the Plague? And why choose the performance of the Passion as your mode of penitence? On the latter point, we can note that Passion Plays had something of a resurgence in the Catholic heartlands of southern Germany and Austria during the previous hundred years. Such plays had started in the twelfth century with many cities across Europe (including Chester and Coventry in England) putting on plays in the Holy Week season. They reached their peak of popularity by around 1500, but then fell out of favour for various reasons. In rural Bavaria, however, they came back into vogue, being seen as a vital part of the Catholic Church reinvigorating the faith of its members. In such a context one might well imagine how the village leaders might make this decision. After all, in their situation of evident suffering and fear, there might be great comfort and consolation in contemplating what had been endured by Jesus, the one they believed to have been none other than the Son of God.

Otto Huber

(The Play's Co-scriptwriter in 2000)

"In recent years, I have been investigating the original texts of the Passion Play. Indeed, I hope very soon to produce a critical edition of the script as it was in 1662.

What I have discovered is fascinating. The 1662 text turns out to be a very careful and creative compilation of two earlier texts—both emanating from the city of Augsburg. One was a medieval text, based on how the Passion Play had been performed in the thirteenth and fourteenth centuries. The other was a revision made in the 1520s by a Protestant.

In this latter version, the writer has made some key changes to the medieval story:

- Not surprisingly, the role of Mary, mother of Jesus, has been radically reduced—indeed she no longer appears in the script at all!
- The role of Judas has been developed, so that the audience is more clearly warned not to emulate his example of betraying Jesus.
- And there are a series of new prologues to each section which helpfully point up the important theological points which the viewer is supposed to detect in the next part of the Play.

What the compiler of the 1662 edition does so masterfully is combine some of these aspects of the Protestant version with other aspects found in the medieval version to produce a powerful and robust text. This was quite an 'ecumenical' achievement! I love to think that the early performances of the Play in the seventeenth century were inspired by such a generous spirit—drawing people together with their different perspectives to find something with which they could each identify in a personal way. For this is a story for everyone!

We must also remember that the first performances of the Play were located in the very cemetery where those who had died in the Plague had been buried. The Play was therefore a dramatic expression of the Christian hope that through identifying with Jesus' death and resurrection, the viewers themselves might pass through death to life. It was a story told in hope of salvation.

There are also other features of the 1662 edition which I much admire:

- The meditation of Mary, holding the dead Jesus on her lap, is very moving. She looks at his hands, through which so many healings had taken place and at his mouth through which he had spoken such powerful messages of truth. In this way, the audience is helped to view Jesus in a new way—through the lens of a mother mourning her son. It is an intuitive and hugely powerful way of contemplating the reality of Jesus.

- There are depictions of the risen Jesus making a special appearance to his mother to bring her the consolation that she so sorely needed.
- There is also a dramatic depiction of Jesus' 'descending into hell' to rescue and redeem those since Adam and Eve who have died without hope.

These are all powerful themes, demonstrating important ways in which the story of Jesus has been received in periods other than our own. The important point to gain from this knowledge of the Play's history, however, is not that we must repeat all these themes in our own day. Rather, we are to find the aspects of the original story which most connect with the concerns of our own generation. That's what they were trying to do in the sixteenth and seventeenth centuries, and we need to be pursuing the same vision in the twenty-first century. We do not change the original story, but we keep seeing fresh aspects of that story which have a contemporary resonance. For this is a story, not just for all people, but for all time!"

The following May (in 1634), the villagers gathered in the church's graveyard to watch over sixty of their fellow-residents perform the first ever Passion Play—"the play of the suffering, death, and resurrection of our Lord Jesus Christ." It has continued ever since. In 1680, the sixth Passion Play was rescheduled to be performed at the start of the decade. During the eighteenth century (the so-called "Age of Reason"), the village had to request permission from political leaders to perform such a "religious" act. This led to the Play sometimes being delayed by a year or, as it was in 1770, to its being banned altogether. Issues of war also have affected the sequence: there was an interrupted season in 1870 and 1871 (due to war with France), a delayed performance in 1922 (because of the First World War), and no performance at all in 1940 (due to the Second World War). Meanwhile there have occasionally been extra seasons introduced: in 1815 (after the end of the Napoleonic Wars) and in 1934 and 1984 (to honour

The village of Oberammergau staged for the Passion Play, colored woodcut by C. E. Doepler (circa 1860)

the three hundredth and three hundred fiftieth anniversaries of the Play). This means the Play in 2020 will be in its forty-second season—surely one of the longest running theatrical performances of all time!

This powerful history makes Oberammergau quite unique—both for its visitors and for its residents. Visitors are introduced to all of the charms of a rural Bavarian village—historic buildings, local shops, places to eat and drink, all set amidst a beautiful surrounding countryside—but in Oberammergau there is something more. The village, having been deeply immersed in the Passion for nearly four hundred years, has been indelibly coloured by this history.

For example, the common Bavarian practice of painting the outside walls of one's house with frescoes (*lüftmalerei* in German) has here been given a biblical twist. Yes, there are frescoes depicting figures from traditional nursery rhymes (such as those on the Hansel and Gretel House),

An aerial view of Oberammergau

but many depict biblical characters. For instance, in those frescoes on the building known as Pilate's House and those on a chemist's shop where the eighteenth-century owner, Franz Zwink, left for passersby an impressive display of characters from the pages of the Bible and the history of the Church.

Also, there is the prominence of woodcarving in the village. If Bethlehem can lay claim to being the unrivaled centre within the Holy Land today for wood-carving, much the same can be said for Oberammergau within Europe. The village supports more than five hundred wood-carvers, whose high-quality work can be seen in so many of the shops. Bethlehem is immersed in the Nativity but Oberammergau in the Passion.

The very number of visitors also makes the village unique. The worldwide fame of the Passion Play causes many tourists to visit every single year but, of course, the number escalates exponentially during the performance season. With potentially up to forty-five hundred people in the audience for each of the five weekly performances and with many of those people wanting to stay the night in the village, Oberammergau is soon brimming to capacity.

Anton (Toni) Preisinger

(Hotel Manager)

"It's quite an experience growing up in Oberammergau. I myself can vividly remember being on stage at the age of two—carried along in the Palm Sunday procession in the arms of my grandfather—and looking up into the face of my father playing the part of a Roman soldier, seated on a horse!

That kind of thing makes a deep impression on a young child. I did not know then that my grandfather had played the role of Jesus in 1950 and 1960, nor that my family had been actively involved in the Play going back for many generations. But, as I grew up, I knew I wanted to play a part in the Play, and twenty years later (after just being in the crowd scenes as a teenager) I was really pleased to be given the role of Archelaus (a junior member in Caiaphas' council). In the following decades, I was given the roles of Judas, then Caiaphas and now, in 2020, the role of Pilate. I'm not quite sure why I am always one of Jesus' opponents. What that say about me? But, it's been very important for me, personally, to be so integrally involved with the Passion Play throughout my life.

Obviously, the Passion Play takes place only once in ten years, but it still affects life in the village in the intervening years. For a start, many of us who have roles in the Play are also involved in putting on other dramatic productions. I've enjoyed being in various Shakespeare plays; and, in the year before the Passion Play, we always stage *Die Pest* (*'The Plague'*), which tells the story of the village being in the grip of the Plague in the year 1633. *Die Pest*, together with the important ceremony in which the villagers actively renew the 1633 vow a few months before the start of the Play, means that we are frequently being reminded of Oberammergau's unique story and are being caught up in that story yet again.

And then, of course, there is the ongoing role we have in welcoming the many visitors to our village. The visitors are not just once every ten years! Every year we are receiving tourists—the museum and the theatre, for example, receive many hundreds of visitors each year. That shows the extraordinary level of interest which people—from all over the world—have in our village because of the Play.

My family has owned a hotel in the heart of the village since 1897. I love giving our visitors a flavour of Bavarian hospitality. During the Passion Play season, however, it can become very hectic! Our hotels need many extra staff, working on a short-term basis; and there's the very high turnaround of guests—staying a maximum of two nights, and sometimes only one.

To be very honest, there are some days when the demands of operating a hotel make the demands of performing in the Play seem the easier of the two! Please don't get me wrong, playing the part of Judas or Caiaphas is, of course, hugely demanding and requires lots of focus. Yet being in the very different world of the first century—just for a few hours—can sometimes come as quite a relief from the pressures of the modern world!

One thing which you quickly become aware of—both on stage or in the village's hotel business—is that there can be quite a contrast between visitors from within Germany and those coming from abroad. The former tend to come as "cultural visitors"—interested in seeing this important part of our German heritage; however, international visitors tend to come more as "religious pilgrims." Obviously there is overlap between the two, but one thing is quite clear: when performing the Play for a predominantly German-speaking audience, you look out on a sea of faces all looking directly towards the stage; but, when performing for an audience which needs constantly to be consulting the English translation, you look out instead on a sea of heads bobbing up and down—each person consulting their Play's translation at a different time to their neighbour!

I do hope the Play continues to be an important part of Oberammergau's life for generations to come. Certainly, within my own family, I know how much my sons (who were aged 12 and 8 when they first saw the Play) began to look ten years ahead and started imagining what part they might play next time round. My oldest son, Anton, will this year be playing the part of the disciple John. Since the oldest son in our family has been called Anton for the last five generations, this probably means this is the fifth Anton Preisinger to be on stage. That's a tradition, I think, that is well worth making the effort to continue!"

All this attention cannot but affect the local residents. What does it feel like to have your small home area "invaded" in this way once every ten years by so many from all around the world? What does it mean to live in a small community which, even if in very positive ways, is seemingly "under the shadow" of the Passion story throughout the intervening years? Above all, what does it mean to go "on stage" with your fellow-villagers and play a small part in the Palm Sunday procession—let alone to be taking one of the twenty main parts, including those of Jesus' mother, Mary Magdalene, or of Jesus himself?

Living in this unique village thus presents its residents with some unique experiences. It was my privilege to meet and talk with some of them in preparing this book. You can see how our conversations developed in the many interviews that have been included—some focusing on life in the village or its history (in this chapter), some on the important work that goes on in the background of the Passion Play's production (in the next chapter, "The Passion on Stage"), and some from those playing key roles on stage (in Part II).

There were others I met whose conversations are not recorded here. On the one hand, some had little direct involvement with the Play or saw it as not affecting their everyday life all that much. Others admitted that

Eva-Maria Reiser and Barbara Schuster

(Both played Mary Magdalene in 2010)

"When the names of the cast went up on the board eighteen months before the 2010 season started, it was really exciting to see both our names there for the role of Mary Magdalene. This is indeed a special role, but for us perhaps even more special—because both of us were already really good friends.

So, during the season we were able to keep encouraging each other, comparing notes and ideas, and processing any criticisms in a constructive way. One of us had a real gift of being positive ('you can do it!'). The other had an ability to trust herself on stage ('don't think about things too much, just do it!'). This really helped us to keep developing our skills and to give of our best throughout the season.

And yet we know that, deep down, we are by nature quite different people. So we weren't trying to get the other to play the role in exactly the same way. It was great to let each other "be herself" in the role—and also to emerge at the end of the season as still really good friends!

During the 2020 season the situation will be slightly different. Eva will play the role of Mary, mother of Jesus, whilst Barbara will continue as Mary Magdalene. However, even in this new role, Eva will still need the same positive attitude which she showed to others when she was Mary Magdalene. And, despite our different roles, we will both be so pleased to be performing in the Play again together."

The people and guests of the town of Oberammergau gather to celebrate the announcement of the cast for the 2020 Passion Play

they saw themselves as standing at some distance from the Christian faith or, if they found themselves being intrigued by the story of Jesus, were still in a critical ongoing dialogue with the Church.

On the other hand, there were those who saw the Passion Play as an important opportunity to help people enter in more deeply to the story of the Gospels. I particularly enjoyed meeting Dr Angelika Winterer, a theologian appointed by the local Catholic archbishop to have a special responsibility for pastoral care and counsel both before and during the Passion Play season. Months before the Play, she was already taking people (through guided reading, listening to short talks, or shared photos of the Holy Land) on meditative journeys to the places and stories described in the Gospels. She was leading many on guided tours around the church (some focused on the *Pestmatrikel*, the Parish Register of Deaths from 1633: see page 19). All of these activities were being designed to help people make the Passion story connect more deeply with their own personal lives.

"Visiting the Passion Play," she commented, "can strengthen people in their faith. This is because the Play tells us how God did not leave Jesus

29

Fr Thomas Gröner

*(Parish Priest of
St. Peter and Paul Church)*

"The residents of Oberammergau have this incredible privilege of going 'inside' the gospel story—of actually living within the 'story of salvation.'

Of course, those people who have grown up here and perhaps performed in the Play during their early childhood may end up taking all this for granted and thus not always appreciate the uniqueness. However, having served in a parish elsewhere in Germany for many years, I can see by comparison how the people here in Oberammergau have a much better knowledge of the Bible.

In my former parish, it was very difficult to talk about Old Testament events such as Moses and the escape from Egypt, but here I soon discovered that they not only know *about* these biblical stories: no, they have actually imagined themselves living *within* these stories. They have seen the tableaux of Moses on stage—some may even have been on that stage—and so they know the story 'in their heart' or 'from the inside out.'

There is also an extra richness to the way we celebrate the events of Holy Week here in the village:

- For example, each year on Palm Sunday we have a processional from the theatre to the church, waving our palm branches, and singing the same hymn which is used to welcome Jesus into Jerusalem in the Passion Play.
- On the evening of Good Friday, it is very special to be focused in our meditations on the depiction of the crucified Christ in the very place where that first vow was made, back in 1633, to perform the Passion Play.

- And at the end of our Paschal Vigil on Holy Saturday, it is wonderful that we can welcome the dawn of Easter Day by singing together the same "Hallelujah" hymn which is the Play's powerful finale.

One of the things I like to ponder is the subtle difference between the Passion Play and our regular liturgical worship. In the former, we in the audience are going *back* in our imaginations to think of the historical Jesus in first-century Jerusalem. In the latter, however, especially as each week we break bread around the Lord's table, we in the congregation experience the risen Jesus coming *forward* towards us! In Italian there is a word *representazione*, which captures this paradox well. The Passion Play is a *representation* of Jesus in the first century; but in our liturgy the risen Jesus is *present* with us, or *'re-presented'* in our midst. So, the Passion Play and the liturgy are working in opposite directions, but in a complementary way which is truly powerful. This way inevitably gives greater depth to our regular Christian worship here in Oberammergau."

alone in the terrible distress of the Passion but ultimately led him through suffering and death to resurrection and life. Moreover, it reminds us how the people of Oberammergau also experienced God's salvation in 1633. Similar experiences can be had by people time and again: they can receive help and assistance whenever they trust in God in their time of need. For this reason the Passion Play can, I truly believe, bring consolation and support, courage, and hope—especially to those who themselves are going through a period of suffering or difficulty."

I also discovered that plans were clearly well in progress for laying on helpful support for visitors during the performance season. Under the overall title of "Experience a Passionate Life," places will be left quiet for personal reflection, communion services will be laid on, and both the Catholic and Lutheran churches will be open throughout the day (for more details see page 9 and the Passion Play's website). There will also be some preseason performances designed specifically for young people.

*The Catholic Church, St. Peter and Paul (left) and the Lutheran
Church, Evangelisch-Lutherische Kirchengemeinde (right)*

All of these plans are designed to help enable the ancient biblical story from two thousand years ago to become real in the present and to help people make their own personal connection with the Passion—to "savour" and taste what they have seen on stage and to "deepen that experience and truly to enter into it for themselves." For to watch the Passion Play indeed presents many in the audience with a unique opportunity themselves to be "immersed in the Passion" in a way which cannot easily be experienced elsewhere.

As you read these interviews, I hope you will find them helping you to feel that you are yourself getting "behind the scene" in some ways and beginning to hear the "inside story" of life in Oberammergau. Meeting these people certainly gave me a new appreciation of the impressive way in which each person has risen to the demanding challenge of putting on this world-famous Passion Play. In many ways, they remain just ordinary people, but what they are able to produce—through their combined efforts and working together—is truly extraordinary. If the village, through its unique history, has indeed come to be "immersed in the Passion," then these residents are working very hard to enable you and the many other visitors who will see the Play to be taken deeper into its meaning.

THE PASSION ON STAGE
Its Power in Performance

It's time for us to go on stage. We have, as it were, been walking around the streets of Oberammergau, sensing how the Passion Play hangs like a mantle over the entire village—creating a special atmosphere in the community. But now, we are going to the theatre itself. What's it like for the residents of this town to put on such a vast performance? In particular in this chapter, what's it like to be one of those in the production team?

In any stage production there are many vital roles being played by those behind the scenes: costume designers, music composers, or scriptwriters. In the next few pages, you will have the opportunity to hear from the Oberammergau residents who are involved in each of these important areas.

Staging, Music, and Colour

Before there can be a play at all, someone has to design the layout of the stage and then construct it. This year, there will be some obvious changes: the stage will be covered by a greater amount of ceiling (enabling more use of electric light during the daylight hours) and there will be a new focus on Jerusalem's temple as a key location for the action. When Carsten Lück, the technical director, took me into the theatre in late August 2019, the stage area was frankly looking far more like a construction site!

Audiences are affected by what they hear and what they see. No stage production can afford to ignore the elements of sound and sight, not just developing strong music but also creating a visual spectacle. Talking with both Markus Zwink (the composer of the music) and Stefan Hageneier (the

Carsten Lück

(Technical Director in 2000, 2010, and 2020)

"Putting on the Passion Play is full of challenges, as you can imagine. There's not just the work to be done in designing and making the costumes, in composing the music, or writing the script; nor just the hard work done by the actors in learning their lines. There is also the big task of designing and then constructing the stage set—not just for the main action but also for the living images or 'tableaux.'

Our set designer, Stefan Hageneier, has done great work on the stage set ever since the 1990 season. This year there will be some significant changes to the main set that will involve months of construction work for my team. Then there's the more detailed work required to create the *tableaux*. In fact, well over a year in advance, Stefan will have already created small, cardboard models for each of these 'Living Images.' He brings them to my office, and we talk through each one—what he's trying to achieve and how. I then look at them and realize, 'I've now got to build each one of these!' That too takes several months. One thing we especially have to ensure is that we get the correct angles and 'elevation' for the audience so they see the scene with appropriate 'perspective.'

We are effectively creating a mini-stage in the middle of the main stage. And, please remember, this mini-stage is strictly temporary. In fact, some *tableaux* are only on stage for a couple of minutes and then immediately need to be replaced by the next one. In 2010, there was one such replacement where we only had seventy-five seconds before the curtain began to pull back—that was quite a rush! We had forty stagehands working as fast as they could to replace the set and then get all the actors into position—quite an achievement!

But the effort—both in the months beforehand and on the day itself—is really worth it. I think the *tableaux* add a really vital extra dimension to the Passion Play. As well as giving the audience some time to process the main action in the scenes, they also give the Passion story its fuller biblical background. If taking a photo of a person, you can add so much to the picture by adding what the photographers call 'depth of field'. That's what the *tableaux* provide for Oberammergau's portrait of Jesus—a 'depth of field' or a historical and theological 'perspective' which helps the audience to come back to the main story with new and deeper insights.

The Passion Play tells a story that is multilayered and offers us a portrait of Jesus who is not 'flat' but multidimensional, and I think the *tableaux* are one of the key ways in which the audience can discover for themselves some of those extra layers and dimensions. To my mind, this then gives the Oberammergau Passion Play, when compared with others, a quality that is quite simply unique."

costume designer) I could sense their creativity, energy, and commitment to this all-encompassing project. Years of hard work and patient reflection will be coming to fruition in 2020.

In my conversations with the production team one of the most exciting things was to be allowed to see the cardboard models which Stefan had made for each of the *tableaux vivants* (or "Living Images"). Here, more than a year in advance, were the precise positions which the actors would need to occupy, standing motionless and still for several minutes! The attention to detail was profound, and the result will no doubt be stunning. Once the vibrant lighting and sheer colour of the costumes is added during the performances, these models will indeed become "living images," full of vitality. The effect should be breath-taking.

These *tableaux* are a distinctive part of Oberammergau's rendition of the Passion Play. Based on various episodes from the Hebrew Scriptures, they give the audience a welcome pause in the action and time to think

One of the tableaux vivants ("Living Images") from the 2010 Passion Play

how Jesus' story is similar to those earlier in Israel's history. Effectively, they give a quiet commentary on the Passion. If in ancient Athens a group of actors forming a chorus would have offered an extended commentary on the unfolding drama of a Greek tragedy, here in Oberammergau we are presented instead with these *tableaux*—visually vibrant and powerfully provocative—which convey their messages in silence. They are likely to be one of your enduring memories of the Play. And spare a thought, too, for Carsten's team who have been constructing these sets for many months but who on the day will be setting them up and then taking them down in such a short space of time!

Writing the Script

Yet there's also another key role—that of the scriptwriter. Although sadly some of the finer points within the script may be lost on us who are not German speakers, we know that a good script is perhaps one of the most important aspects of any play.

It's no easy task. Being a scriptwriter for a comedy or a modern fictional drama poses many challenges, but these are only increased when one is

Stefan Hageneier

(Set & Costume Designer in 2000, 2010, & 2020)

"I so enjoyed designing the stage set and the costumes in 2000 and 2010. However, after the 2010 season I said to myself, 'I don't think I can do this again!' The Passion Play season is so intense. You never stop thinking about it from one moment to the next! Later, however, I got some energy back and thought I *could* perhaps do it once more, and I began to come up with some fresh ideas.

This time you will see quite a difference with the staging. We have created a single set for the whole Play which shows the doors of the temple. The temple was, after all, the single most dominant feature in Jerusalem, and its opulence caused Jesus' disciples to feel quite overawed by contrast with their experience of village-life in Galilee. There was a sense in which all Jesus' activity was seen in some kind of relation to this enormous building.

Meanwhile, for the two indoor scenes which were *not* located near the temple (when Jesus was in Bethany and at the Last Supper) there will be a tent on stage. This tent allows us to portray this darker "indoor space" for both those events which took place after sunset. Yet visually, this tent will be in front of the temple. The Gospel writers, so I understand, were often drawing an implicit contrast between Jesus and the temple (itself built to remember the Hebrews' 'tent of meeting' in the Exodus story). I will be fascinated to see what effect this new staging design has on the audience as they too consider the whole story of Jesus through the 'lens,' as it were, of the temple.

As for the costumes, there will be some differences here too. In 2010 there was a lot of colour (Romans in red, Hebrews in blue) and some very distinctive headgear. It was quite theatrical! This time I've gone for a historical emphasis with more muted colours.

I'm hoping this will give the whole Play a tone which is more serious and realistic.

I have also had new ideas for the *tableaux*. The *tableaux* are such an important part of the Passion Play. I've highlighted some of their common themes—in particular, the abusive power and decadent wealth of the rulers (in Egypt or Babylon) and the Hebrews' refugee status as they experienced being cast out and homeless. In both these areas, connections can be made to the story of Jesus and also to our own day.

Yet, for me, perhaps the most fascinating insight came to me while I was preparing the *tableaux's* balsa-wood models. I suddenly realized that these stories from the Hebrew Scriptures would have been well known to Jesus himself. He would have been able to compare what was happening to him with what had happened to Joseph, Moses, and Daniel, and from these historical images, he could derive new strength for the challenges ahead. Seen in this way, the *tableaux* give us a window into the mindset of Jesus, an imaginative *entrée* into his thought-world, and an opportunity to be inspired by what inspired him. The *tableaux*, though strictly silent, really do have a 'voice' of their own—speaking louder than words!"

seeking to put on stage any event from real history. How does one ensure the performance is true to the facts when it is a "performance"—an artificial and slightly contrived creation? How does one accurately convey some of the emotions involved? And if, as the scriptwriter, you have a particular point of view you want to convey, how do you do that? By contrast, book writers can add so much in their own voice—giving geographical or historical information or expressing the private inner thoughts of those in the action—but as a scriptwriter for a stage production your options are far more limited.

Matters become even more complex when the play is about more distant events from history. Hundreds of years later, we know just the top-level facts. All we can see at this distance in time is the "tip of an iceberg": most of the original history—what was really happening "on the streets"—now lies buried out of view. How can you help the audience imagine themselves inside such an ancient story? Presumably, you will have to write something which is humanly credible and makes sense—even though, strictly, it is fictitious. For the only way to convey historical truth on stage is to write a script that is based on imagination. In one sense, the script is imaginary but, at another level, it is conveying truth. Indeed, when one stops to think about it, this use of the imagination is the only way that a script can become "authentic" in the experience of the audience. Only then can it *feel real*.

All of these issues inevitably confront those writing the script for a Passion Play. However, the potential difficulties are even greater. For a start, this story is set much further back in time. The audience will need to be taken on an imaginary journey of "time travel" going back through two thousand years. They need to be transported from the modern world into the ancient Roman Empire and indeed into a very strange smaller "sub-world" within that—the world of first-century Judaism. How can they step "into the shoes" of a first-century Jew? And, can the audience ever get inside their minds, adopting a Jewish worldview? There is a real challenge here to help people adjust their mindsets.

Despite the distance in time, with a Passion Play there is one striking advantage—we know far more about that week in Jerusalem than any other week in ancient history. It's not just that we now have good archaeological evidence of first-century Jerusalem and have good sources on what the Passover celebrations would have been like. We also have four accounts of what happened on the Sunday, the Monday, the Thursday, the Friday, and the following Sunday! Moreover, the story is told from the perspective, not of later imperial historians, but of real people on the ground. In other words, we know something of what was being talked about "on the streets"!

Yet this comparative wealth of down-to-earth information can also cause some difficulties for the scriptwriter of a Passion Play. For a start,

The Passion Play Theatre during set construction for the 2020 season

given that there are four different Gospels, does one give a preference to one of those four accounts and its particular "angle" on Jesus? And, although we know the names of some of the ordinary "bit players" (such as Peter, Thomas, and Mary), we can often only guess at what they were really feeling as they went through these dramatic events. The scriptwriter is still going to have to embellish the original account quite considerably.

At that point, one runs into another difficulty. This particular story is sacred to so many and the very language of the original accounts has become canonical and revered. How can one add to the Bible—the historic script—without in some way being thought to undermine it? Moreover, many in the audience will be very familiar with this story or even devoted to it—seeing it as a foundational story within their faith and spirituality. How can one help them discover new and even shocking insights into the original story without causing offence?

Suddenly we realize that the task of writing the script for a Passion Play is no easy task. Other plays may present challenges of how to convey authentic history in an imaginable and authentic way, but here there

Otto Huber
(The Play's Co-Scriptwriter in 2000)

"It was an incredible privilege to be involved in adapting the script for the Passion Play for the 2000 season. Over the years, various elements had been introduced into the script which did require a thorough reexamination. For example, there were medieval caricatures of the Jewish people as greedy for money and other things which, in the light of the tragic events of the twentieth century, could rightly now be deemed "anti-Semitic."

So, with the help and advice of historians and theologians, we made some significant changes to the script compiled by Joseph Alois Daisenberger in the 1860s:

- We highlighted the key fact that Jesus himself was thoroughly Jewish.
- We indicated that Judas' motives may well have been not commercial but religious or political.
- We introduced the singing of the *Shema* (the daily-recited Jewish prayer based on Deuteronomy), and we ensured it was sung in Hebrew by the Jewish crowds in the temple.
- We emphasized that there were some of the Jewish Sanhedrin (such as Joseph of Arimathea) who disapproved of the high priest's actions.
- We made it clear that Jesus' death ultimately came about not only because of the Jewish leaders but because of all of us.

Historically this was indeed a Jewish story, but in another important sense it proves also to be a universal story—indeed *the* universal story—in which the sins and failings of all of us are exposed and revealed.

> The Passion story thus provides a window into all our hearts. Some commentators on the Play two hundred years ago described the purpose of the Play in this way: the viewer is to look and to listen; to confess their own shortcomings; and then to be moved to a new love for God, for Jesus, and for all our fellow human beings in this world marked by so much suffering.
>
> There are other plays which seem to have the purpose of encouraging the audience to take revenge, but that should be the very last thing provoked in those who are immersing themselves in the true story of Jesus. It calls us instead to self-reflection, to gratitude for Jesus' suffering, and to a renewed heart of love."

are issues that touch on spiritual faith and personal commitments. A Passion Play, by the very nature of its subject matter, can never only be about history. It also includes that potentially most divisive of subjects— theology. For the Gospel writers were not just "bare historians," they were committed Christian believers. They presented a story which, for them, was not just historically true but theologically extraordinary.

How does the scriptwriter of a Passion Play juggle these inevitable issues of theology? For example, if the Gospel writers advance the claim that Jesus was not just a remarkable human being but also mysteriously embodied the character of Israel's God, how can a Passion Play give appropriate space for that conclusion to be drawn? Must the focus be solely on the "historical Jesus" or can the script include words that point to the "divinity" of Jesus? And, if the Gospel writers assert that this historical Jesus was physically raised from the dead, how does one portray such a "miracle" on stage? Or, is it best to convey this idea in more symbolic ways, giving space for the audience to draw their own conclusions?

For nearly four hundred years those producing the Passion Play in Oberammergau have been wrestling with these and other similar issues. In the early years, there were issues to do with blending Catholic and Reformed perspectives on the Passion. In 1730, allegorical characters were introduced by the Augustinian Anselm Manhart—setting the Passion story against the backdrop of a battle between Jesus and Satan (together with his minions: Jealousy, Avarice, Sin, and Death). Then during the Age of Reason, the Play went in a different, more meditative, direction with the Benedictine Ferdinand Rosner introducing the *tableaux vivants*. In the 1810s, a new script by Othmar Weis eliminated any allegorical elements, focused on the realism of the Gospels, used prose rather than verse, and began to highlight moral issues such as social injustice. In 1860, the text was revised again by a man called Josef Alois Daisenberger, who focused more on idealism and on the psychological elements in the story. One hundred year later, as we come into our own times, we find that Daisenberger's text is still being used from the 1960s onward but real care is now being taken to ensure that the text is free from any implied anti-Semitism.

Throughout the last three hundred eighty years, we can see how the script of the Play has necessarily been influenced by the important concerns of each particular era—concerns both in the Christian church and also in the wider world of politics and philosophy. Each scriptwriter has sought to make fresh and vital connections between this ancient story and the contemporary world. The script has constantly evolved as it has traveled down the line of human history.

In 2020, it will be no different. Indeed for this coming season we will have the privilege of experiencing a script created by a director who has been wrestling with these issues—back and forth—for over thirty years. To sit with Christian Stückl, as I did for five hours, to witness his creative energy, and to feel his passion, was itself an eye-opening experience— seeing so many fascinating issues flowing through his fertile imagination. I expect some things in his eventual script will no doubt be a mixture of the classically familiar and the surprisingly novel. Yet, that's precisely the way in which this ancient story can come and meet us in fresh and exciting ways.

The Passion Play is about to begin. Let's take our seats!

Christian Stückl

(Director in 1990, 2000, 2010, and 2020)

"One of the challenges in producing the Play has been the increasing lack of prior knowledge about the biblical story among the younger generation. Perhaps forty years ago, one could presume a basic familiarity with the story of Jesus, but now, it seems we are often dealing with a 'clean sheet of paper.' One of the exciting results is that actors are far more likely to come up with entirely fresh perspectives.

I love these fresh perspectives on this ancient, historical story. My focus when directing is not primarily on the possible effect that the Play will have on the audience. Instead, I am trying to help each actor to grow in their understanding of the character of the person they are enacting. If they are really able to get inside that character, to think and feel as they did, then I know the portrayal will have the power to communicate itself immediately to the audience.

To put this another way, I want the actors to use their imagination as human beings, thinking how ordinary people would have reacted even in these extraordinary circumstances—because *that* is what will help the audience too to imagine themselves in that situation. We human beings, for all our obvious differences, are remarkably the same in our emotions—across both time and space—and it's this, our common humanity, which pulls the audience fully back into the historical drama.

This focus on the actor's imagination means that sometimes during rehearsals, as he or she begins to inhabit the role more instinctively, the actor begins to come up with new lines of script which better express what the character might have said in that situation. I'm very happy with this development—these are the new perspectives I love!

In that sense this means the text is 'open' throughout the rehearsal season and only becomes the finished script some four weeks or so before the premier performance (time enough for the English translator to finish its work). I love to see the actors wrestling hard with my initial text, trying to make it their own, but then offering improvements to it—thereby making it even more truly their own!

Yet there's another aspect that comes to the fore uniquely in Oberammergau's performance of the Passion Play. Since 1980, we have always had two different actors assigned to each of the major roles. The dual actors make eminent sense over a long five-month season—otherwise they would soon become exhausted! However, it means that the same role may be performed in two quite different ways. This possibility gives each performance a distinctive quality—it is never quite the same as the day before! It also reveals the reality that each of us has a unique character. Even when we are performing an identical script for an identical role, we will each 'make it our own' in our own distinctive way.

Finally, one has to note that this deliberate focus on using our historical imagination and on our common humanity inevitably has some effect on the way this Passion Play portrays the character of Jesus. Those people who confess the creeds of the catholic church will naturally come to this play motivated by their conviction that Jesus was the divine 'Son of God.' Yet that conviction should never be threatened by also seeing the full humanity of Jesus.

That's why the Play seeks to portray not just the last few days of Jesus' Passion, but also (by including his words spoken earlier in the Gospels) the whole of his ministry—not just his dying, we might say, but also his living. That's why, by using our imagination, we seek to portray Jesus as a first-century Jew (which he was) and as a credible human being (which he was too). In this way, we hope, the authentic Jesus of history becomes intelligible to a larger number of people and the door of faith can be held open to a much wider audience, many of whom otherwise might never have bothered to consider this remarkable character from ancient history, Jesus of Nazareth."

More Scenes from the *PASSION PLAY!*

PART II
Experiencing the Play

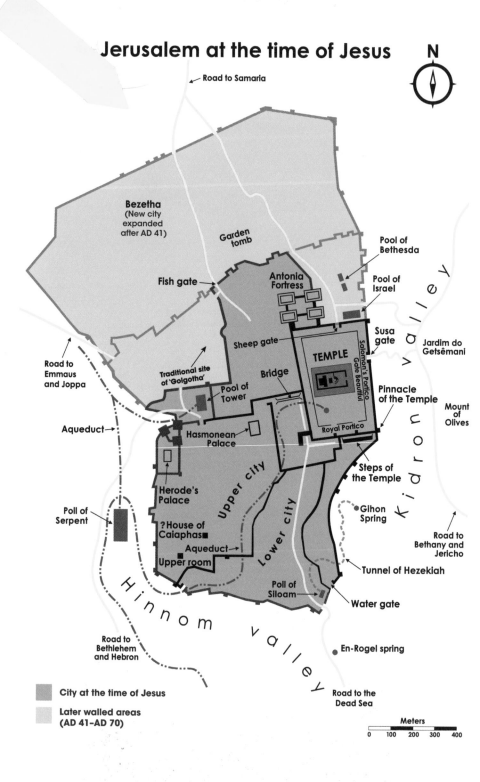

Jerusalem at the time of Jesus

N

Road to Samaria

Bezetha
(New city
expanded
after AD 41)

Garden
tomb

Pool of
Bethesda

Fish gate

Antonia
Fortress

Pool of
Israel

Susa
gate

Jardim do
Getsêmani

Sheep gate

TEMPLE

Road to
Emmaus
and Joppa

Traditional site
of 'Golgotha'

Bridge

Pool of
Tower

Salomon's Portico
Gate Beautiful

Pinnacle
of the Temple

Mount
of
Olives

Aqueduct

Hasmonean
Palace

Royal Portico

Steps of
the Temple

Upper city

Herode's
Palace

Gihon
Spring

Road to
Bethany and
Jericho

Poll of
Serpent

?House of
Caiaphas

Lower city

Aqueduct

Upper room

Tunnel of Hezekiah

Poll of
Siloam

Water gate

Hinnom valley

Kidron valley

Road to
Bethlehem
and Hebron

En-Rogel spring

Road to the
Dead Sea

City at the time of Jesus

Later walled areas
(AD 41–AD 70)

Meters

0   100   200   300   400

THE PASSION PLAY
2020

Jesus Arrives in Jerusalem

SUNDAY

Act I: Jesus Enters Jerusalem

They say that, to this day, any Jewish heart when it catches a first sighting of Jerusalem "misses a beat"—such is the Jewish depth of affection for this city at the centre of their national story.

It would have been on that memorable day when Jesus made his so-called "Triumphal Entry." The many Galilean pilgrims, who had been walking for the last week in Jesus' company, would instinctively have had a rush of joy and delight when—at last—they came over the crest of the Mount of Olives and saw the beauty of their mother-city spread out before their eyes.

> When he came near the place where the road goes down the Mount of Olives, the whole crowd of disciples began joyfully to praise God in loud voices for all the miracles they had seen:
>
> "Blessed is the king who comes in the name of the Lord!"
>
> "Peace in heaven and glory in the highest!"
>
> (Luke 19:37-38)

The last part of their journey had been a long climb through the desert, coming up from Jericho (near the Dead Sea, the lowest place on the face of the planet) to Jerusalem, itself over 2,700 feet above sea level. Presumably, they had set out at the break of dawn in order to cover the necessary fourteen miles in one day. Not surprisingly, we read in Mark's Gospel that by the time Jesus reached Jerusalem it was "already late" in the afternoon. It had been a long day, and the pilgrims would have been tired but also filled with a sense of arrival and expectation. Now they could settle down and start preparing for the Passover festival!

This particular year, they had other reasons for their excitement. They all had high hopes for this Jesus-figure, this powerful teacher from Nazareth, this prophet in their midst. Might some sparks begin to fly once they hit Jerusalem?! Luke expressly says that there were many amongst the pilgrims setting out from Jericho who thought, as Jesus neared Jerusalem, that the "kingdom of God was going to appear at once." They were on tip-toe with expectation. Might this be the year when, through this Jesus, God's kingly rule over Israel might be restored? Would those hated oppressors, the Romans, at last be removed from the land?!

Jesus himself, however, seemed to have some other ideas. As the pilgrims set out through the Judean desert, he told them a parable about a king coming back to his own country and judging those who during his absence had rebelled. What was Jesus driving at? From their perspective the idea of Jesus as a king was indeed good news, but why did he describe his coming as a "return"? Why was he speaking about judgment?

When they came up the final slopes of the Mount of Olives, Jesus requisitioned a donkey from the nearby village of Bethany. Why a donkey and not something more impressive? Why not a horse or a mighty stallion? If the Romans ever got to hear about this supposed "king" approaching on a silly donkey, they would be moved to pitiable laughter—or even outright scorn!

What few people in the crowd that day realized, however, was that Jesus was deliberately evoking an ancient prophecy from their Hebrew Scriptures: "Rejoice greatly, Daughter Zion!…See, your king comes to you…lowly and riding on a donkey, on a colt, the foal of a donkey" (Zechariah 9:9). His entry into Jerusalem was evidently in Jesus' own mind

Living Image 1:
The Loss of Paradise

Genesis 3:22-24

The LORD God said, "The man has now become like one of us, knowing good and evil. He must not be allowed to reach out his hand and take also from the tree of life and eat, and live forever." So the LORD God banished him from the Garden of Eden.... After he drove the man out, he placed on the east side of the Garden of Eden cherubim and a flaming sword flashing back and forth to guard the way to the tree of life.

These words conclude the Bible's foundational story. Adam and Eve, who in Genesis 2 were portrayed as enjoying life in a beautiful garden, created by God, now find themselves—as a result of disobeying God's clear instructions not to eat from the "tree of the knowledge of good and evil"—banished from God's presence. Is there any way back?

This banishment then sets up one of the major plotlines in the entire Bible. Is there a way back to the "tree of life"? to the Garden of Eden? to the enjoyment of God's blessing? And, now that all our human relationships seem so evidently to be marred by tension and prone to breakdown, is there any way that love, trust, and peace can be restored between us?

Eventually, as the Bible's dramatic plot unfolds, there appears on the scene a person who seems to embody God's presence and his love, who restores relationships, and who mysteriously ends up dying on a wooden cross—described later by his followers as a "tree." Could this be the beginning of the way back? Is Jesus, through all the ugliness of the Passion which reveals the very worst that we human beings can do to each other, actually working to a deeper script—doing something which will overturn the sin of Adam and Eve?

Scene of Jesus entering Jerusalem from the 2010 Passion Play

a moment not for the forcing of a political agenda but for the fulfillment of prophecy.

Jesus was indeed coming into Jerusalem as its king. Simon Peter had been right to blurt out his suspicion—that Jesus was the "Messiah," the royal anointed King of Israel. Bartimaeus, on the outskirts of Jericho, had been right to keep shouting out that Jesus was the "Son of David"—the long-awaited successor to Jerusalem's first and greatest king. We might well imagine some in the crowd singing, "Hail to you, hail to you, oh David's son! The throne of the fathers is due to you!"

Yet this was a king with a difference. On the one hand, he would turn out to be—at least in the eyes of some, such as perhaps Judas Iscariot—so much less than he could have been. This king would not attempt to banish the Romans and that longed-for independent kingdom of Israel would not dawn on the political horizon. Such ardent nationalism would be cruelly disappointed.

On the other hand, he would turn out to be—at least in the eyes of his later followers, such as Simon Peter and Mary Magdalene—so much more than they had ever expected even in their wildest dreams. This king turned out to be indeed a "returning" king—precisely what the prophet Isaiah had foreseen would be the cause of Jerusalem's greatest joy:

> *How beautiful on the mountains / are the feet of those who bring good news…who say to Zion, / "Your God reigns!"…When the LORD returns to Zion,… Burst into songs of joy together, / you ruins of Jerusalem; / for the LORD has comforted his people, / he has redeemed Jerusalem (Isaiah 52:7-9).*

Christian Stückl

(Director in 1990, 2000, 2010, and 2020)

"Most Passion Plays begin with the so-called 'Triumphal Entry' as Jesus comes over the Mount of Olives and makes his way into Jerusalem surrounded by the many pilgrims from Galilee. It certainly makes for a dramatic start! In Oberammergau there is the added factor that so many of the local villagers—men, women, and children—are coming onto the stage and welcoming Jesus as he rides on his donkey. It's quite a spectacle and understandably provides the audience with some of its most vivid memories of the whole Play.

In the Gospels, Jesus' followers are calling out, 'Blessed is the coming kingdom of our father David! Hosanna in the highest!' (Mark 11:10). Since the early 1800s, the Oberammergau crowds have entered singing Rochus Dedler's hymn: *'Heil dir, Heil dir, o Davids Sohn!'* (*'Hail to you, Hail to you, oh David's Son!'*). This hymn has become a much-loved local anthem which we have all learnt since our childhood. It's strong, formal, and majestic.

Yet I can't help but thinking that the original Palm Sunday would have been far more chaotic. It was, after all, a spontaneous, unplanned moment of excitement. In proclaiming the 'coming kingdom of David,' the crowds clearly saw this occasion not just as a religious moment but also as a political one. If we had been there on that day, we might well have felt we were getting involved not just in a religious pageant but perhaps even in a political demonstration!

The next verse in Mark's Gospel makes it clear that Jesus went into the temple, but 'since it was already late, he went out to Bethany' (11:11). We often wrongly imagine that Jesus stormed straight into the temple in order to drive out the money-changers. But the reality was quite different.

By the way, Jesus' leaving the temple so quickly is important within the Play for dramatic reasons. The audience can be transported to Bethany and be introduced in a more private setting to the individual character of Jesus' followers—not just the twelve male disciples but his female followers (including Mary Magdalene) and also Jesus' mother and his family. We begin to hear their different fears and hopes, their divergent agendas for the future, their varied responses to Jesus. This sets up some important subthemes for the rest of the Play, as we see each character react differently to the events unfolding around him or her.

Jesus' leaving the temple in this way—without immediately moving into a mode of condemnation—is even more important for the Play's overall message and its major plotline. In the early 1900s, the Play's basic plot was that Jesus had so outraged the greedy money-lenders in the temple that they immediately started demanding Jesus' death. This was not a good way to start! Not only did it easily foster and endorse some negative stereotypes of Jewish people, but it was also contrary to the evidence—that Jesus' death came about for a variety of reasons. First-century Jerusalem was a veritable vortex of religious and political tensions—brewing with so many different agendas—that a unique figure like Jesus was bound to be treading on many different toes!

That's why in our portraying Jesus' return to the temple in Act III, we deliberately have some time whilst we hear Jesus' teaching from the Law of Moses and upholding the importance of mercy and loving-kindness. Only later, when this provokes a negative response, does Jesus begin to move to words of judgment and then the overturning of the money-changers' tables.

I was also determined to show how Jesus, who called the temple a 'house of prayer', actually himself prayed in the temple! Hence the great new musical moment, when we hear Jesus and those on stage all singing the *Shema Yisrael* prayer in Hebrew! (see page 41) Jesus was, after all, a good Jew!

Finally, in these opening scenes we see the ways in which the tableaux start to focus on the Old Testament figure of Moses. In times past, some of these tableaux used to focus on Joseph being betrayed by his brothers (which again could be given some unfortunate interpretations), but now we've deliberately focused on the one whom the Jewish people looked back to as their greatest leader.

This new focus enables us to see Jesus in very Jewish terms and as a latter-day Moses: leading God's people to freedom, performing a new Exodus, and teaching a new law. Sometimes people draw too sharp a contrast between Jesus and the Old Testament, but Jesus himself said that he had 'not come to abolish them [the Law] but rather to fulfill [it]' (Matthew 5:17). So, it's really important, as the Play develops, for the audience to recognize that Jesus is not opposed to all the Mosaic religion that has gone before —as it were, overturning all the tables— but rather is seeking to bring it to its true fulfillment. Jesus may be doing a new thing, but he remains firmly Jewish and fully faithful to his Hebrew tradition.

In these various ways, these opening three acts, together with the tableaux, are introducing the audience to a variety of themes. It's like a complex and tightly woven tapestry drawing together so many strands of human experience. This, I hope, makes for a far more interesting telling of the Passion story—but also one that is far more likely to be closer to the original multilayered drama that was actually played out in first-century Jerusalem.

As the audience now joins in following this drama, I hope their interest and intrigue has been aroused—to see how things develop. Yes, they may think they know the main story quite well, but what about the detail? And, despite being familiar with the Passion story, are they ready to gain fresh insights into its many undercurrents and subplots? For the action in the Play is about to become a whole lot more complex. As I believe you say in English, 'the plot thickens'! Let's go on a journey together to see what happens next!"

Jesus in Bethany & Temple

MONDAY to WEDNESDAY

Act II: Jesus in Bethany

From Bethany there are great views of the sun rising over the Dead Sea and the wilderness of Judea. Perched on the slopes of the Mount of Olives, Bethany in Jesus' day was still only a tiny village—being the last possible outpost of human habitation before the arid desert soil to the east made vegetation impossible. As such, it was the perfect place to get away from the bustle and stress of the busy city of Jerusalem—located out of sight on the other side of the Mount.

Almost certainly, this is where Jesus and his twelve male disciples slept those first few nights. Each day he would commute into town, teaching in the temple, but in the evening, he could retreat to this quiet haven. Quite possibly, these thirteen men were given accommodation in several different homes—after all, they may not all have been able to fit into the home where Lazarus, Martha, and Mary lived. On one evening, they evidently took their meal together in the home of a man whom Mark calls "Simon the leper" (quite possibly someone whom Jesus had healed of that dreaded disease). Yet what happened next took them by surprise, "a woman came with an alabaster jar of very expensive perfume, made of pure nard. She broke the jar and poured the perfume on his head" (Mark 14:3).

In John's Gospel, the woman is explicitly named as Mary, the sister of Lazarus (John 11:2; 12:3). Some have been suspicious as to why Mark has left her anonymous. However, this may have been for a very practical reason: to reveal her name would put Mary at risk from reprisals during her lifetime (whereas by the time John's Gospel came to be written, she had since died). Though the debate continues, this "Mary of Bethany" is arguably to be identified also with the "Mary Magdalene" who was first mentioned in Luke 8:2—immediately after a story of a woman shedding her tears and pouring some perfume over Jesus' feet.

Living Image 2:
Moses Leads the Israelites through the Red Sea

Exodus 14:10, 13, 21-22

As Pharaoh approached, the Israelites looked up, and there were the Egyptians, marching after them. They were terrified and cried out to the LORD. Moses answered the people, "Do not be afraid. Stand firm and you will see the deliverance the LORD will bring you today." Then Moses stretched out his hand over the sea, and all that night the LORD drove the sea back with a strong east wind… The waters were divided, and the Israelites went through the sea on dry ground, with a wall of water on their right and on their left.

Of the five tableaux which involve the figure of Moses, this first one highlights that definitive moment when Moses bravely leads the Israelites through the separated water of the "Sea of Reeds." Once safely on the eastern shore, they will look back and sing together of God's great rescue from the hands of the evil ruler of Egypt, the Pharaoh: "I will sing to the Lord, for he is highly exalted. The Lord is my strength and my defense; he has become my salvation."

By the time Jesus came to Jerusalem this divine rescue had been remembered annually for many centuries in the festival of Passover. Those in the city that week looked back to Moses as their great leader and saviour, the one through whom God had rescued them from a dreaded political tyrant and brought them into a safe place where they could worship him freely. How they hoped God would do that again!

Jesus would indeed, like Moses, need to trust in God in the face of enemy threats and real opposition; but he seemed to have a different agenda. His followers would later look back and conclude that he had been performing a new and deeper "exodus"—forging a narrow "escape route" through the deep waters of death and out the other side. This Jesus (whose very name meant "God saves") had for them indeed "become their salvation."

If so, this same woman is now in Bethany performing a very similar action—but this time with a deeper purpose. In Galilee her action may have been an uncontrollable expression of her gratitude to Jesus for his rescuing her from her sinful past, an expression of her love for having received Jesus' forgiveness (hence Jesus' comment in Luke 7:47, "whoever has been forgiven little loves little"). Now in Bethany, it's something more.

Some wonder if it's just a coincidence that the only other references in the Bible to "nard" or "spikenard" (an oil from a plant native to the Himalayas) come in the Old Testament's "love song," the Song of Songs: "while the king was his table, / my perfume spread its fragrance" (1:12; cf. 4:13). Mary's action does not need to be explicitly "sexual" in order for us to acknowledge that this is a powerful expression of love addressed from a woman towards a man. This is the nearest, we might say, that Jesus will ever get to experiencing his own wedding and being celebrated (like the kings of old in Psalm 45) as a human bridegroom.

Others rightly wonder if Mary's anointing the head of Jesus was her way of giving Jesus his deserved "coronation" as Israel's true King (after all, the word *Messiah* means the "anointed one"). If so, it was a remarkable act—and one that might indeed put Mary in danger from the religious authorities.

Jesus discerns in her symbolic action something even more profound: "she did what she could. She poured perfume on my body beforehand to prepare for my burial" (Mark 14:8). Jesus is not just Mary's beloved, not just her king, but also the one who would be dying for her. This event is not just akin to a royal wedding but also to a funeral. It is indeed beautiful, but it is also slightly bizarre.

Mary, operating with an intuitive understanding that leaves the male disciples lagging far behind, has picked up some unspoken signals from Jesus and has now fathomed where he is headed. Behind all the outward and public celebrations, as seen in his recent triumphant entrance into the city, she has detected an inner, private theme of tragedy and looming death. A drama is being unfolded in which she has discovered—ahead of all the others—the inner plotline. She will go through the next few days with this extra, crushing, level of insight. When a few days later her intuitions are vindicated and her worst fears confirmed, not surprisingly, she will wish so desperately to be the first one to anoint Jesus' body and embalm his precious corpse—now for the third and final time.

ACT III: Expulsion of the Temple Merchants— Pilate and Caiaphas—Judas and High Council

If Bethany was the place of quiet and private retreat, then the temple was the place of powerful and public action. This enormous building-complex was the very epicentre of Jewish life—its religious heartbeat but also its political hub as well. The temple was where Jewish worshipers might come on a daily basis. It was where Jewish pilgrims would throng at each of their four annual festivals. It was also (as we learn from Josephus' writings) where Jewish nationalists would gather throughout these tense decades in Judaism's standoff with Rome. The temple was the place where riots could develop quickly, causing the Roman soldiers to storm onto the premises from the nearby Antonia fortress in order to quell the unrest. In other words, it was the place where sparks could fly. Seemingly small actions could have devastating consequences. It would not take much to set the whole thing ablaze.

Located on the site of Solomon's first temple (dedicated around 970 BC), the whole area had been experiencing a massive renovation programme throughout the last 45 years. Around the year 20 BC, Herod the Great had commissioned a vast expansion of the temple's platform requiring enormous stones to be hauled in from nearby quarries in order to constitute the platform's supporting walls. This expansion of the level area on the top meant that there was now around the inner sanctuary a large area known as the "Court of the Gentiles"—something which, as a non-Jew, Herod might have hoped one day to enjoy himself.

Jesus' cleansing of the temple [during the 2010 Passion Play]

But how was this new "court of the Gentiles" to be used? The high priests had recently allowed a market to develop here. After all, worshipers needed to exchange their ordinary money into the temple's unique currency (the Tyrian shekel) and then use that money to pay for their sacrificial offerings and to make any extra financial gifts towards the temple's construction and daily operation. All these necessary actions had to be conducted somewhere. Why not here?

Jesus disagreed. Returning to the temple the day after his first arrival, Jesus entered its courts:

> *Jesus entered the temple courts and began driving out those who were buying and selling there. He overturned the tables of the money changers and the benches of those selling doves, and would not allow anyone to carry merchandise through the temple courts. And as he taught them, he said, "Is it not written: 'My house will be called a house of prayer for all nations'? But you have made it 'a den of robbers.'"*
>
> *(Mark 11:15-17)*

This famous event, often termed Jesus' "cleansing of the temple," is widely agreed—even amongst radical scholars who are otherwise dismissive of what the Gospels record—as an indisputable event in the ministry of the historical Jesus and indeed the single most important "trigger" which precipitated his death. How did he dare to do this? "By what authority," the religious authorities are very soon asking, "are you doing do these things? And who gave you authority to do this?" (Mark 11:28). In other words, we might say, "who on earth do you think you are?"

Living Image 3:
The Ten Commandments and the Dance around the Golden Calf

Exodus 32:1, 3-4, 6

When the people saw that Moses was so long in coming down from the mountain, they gathered around Aaron and said, "Come, make us gods who will go before us." So all the people took off their earrings and brought them to Aaron. He took what they handed him and made it into an idol cast in the shape of a calf. Then they said, "These are your gods, Israel, who brought you up out of Egypt."

This extraordinary episode comes in the very midst of the Exodus story. Within that grand story—the foundational story within the Hebrew Scriptures—the God of Israel has displayed his love and power through rescuing his people from slavery in Egypt. And he is now about to reveal his character and truth through giving the Ten Commandments to Moses, when suddenly the Israelites turn aside from this God to worship a golden calf. They turn from serving the living and active God to worshiping this inanimate and powerless idol—a creation of their own hands. Their inner hearts are exposed. And, worse still, this is all instigated by Aaron, the one who will be God's appointed priest.

As Jesus goes into the temple, the same issue of idolatry comes to the surface. The temple was supposed to be the very place appointed by the God of Israel to be the "place of his Name," the place where there was a celebration of his law given at Sinai; but going back at least to the era of Jeremiah, the Hebrew prophets recognized that it could paradoxically become a place of idolatry.

So Jesus issues a challenge—calling people back to the worship of the living God. Yet, it soon appears, there are those—shockingly from amongst the temple's leading officials and priests—who may have their hearts set on things other than God—on financial extortion, on external religious rituals, or on personal or political power. It's a sharp moment of revelation, exposing the inner hearts of all.

From the Hebrew Scriptures an understanding had developed that there was an intrinsic link between the king and the temple. Just as David and Solomon had planned and built the temple, so it would be David's ultimate successor, the Messiah, who would rebuild or bring about the longed-for restoration of the temple. Evidently Herod, despite his exalted self-importance and his title as the "king of the Jews," had not really been the Messiah. But was Jesus now performing this action in order to make his own alternative claim to be the authentic Messiah?

Almost certainly, making his own claim is indeed precisely what Jesus was doing. Yes, he was concerned about financial exploitation of the poor. Yes, he was angry that Gentiles could not have a less commercially driven location in which to worship and were forced to pray amidst the noise and evil of a "den of robbers" (a phrase drawn from Jeremiah's dire predictions that Solomon's temple would soon be destroyed). Yet Jesus was also making a point about himself. He was the one with the ultimate authority over the temple. Not coincidentally, he started quoting the words of God himself, as conveyed through the prophecy of Isaiah, "My house…" Was he implying that this "house," this temple, really belonged to him?!

In the opening verses of Mark's Gospel, the evangelist had quoted a verse from the prophet Malachi (3:1) to help his readers understand who Jesus was. "I will send my messenger, who will prepare the way before me," the verse had begun (and Mark saw this as a reference to John the Baptist as the "messenger" who came before Jesus). Yet, the verse continued, "then suddenly the Lord you are seeking will come to his temple." For this Gospel-writer there may be many different layers of meaning beneath the "temple cleansing" (a criticism of commercial wrong-doing, a concern for Gentile access to God, even a warning that the temple's days were numbered, as in the days of Jeremiah), but this layer too was not to be missed—Jesus came into the temple as the "Lord" predicted by Malachi, as its rightful owner. Like a landlord returning to his tenant farm or vineyard, he was looking for faithfulness and fruitfulness, but that, tragically, was not what he found.

Barbara Schuster

(Mary Magdalene in 2010 & 2020)

"One of the key things which impressed me so much through playing the role of Mary Magdalene was her ability to carry on with her positive faith in Jesus, regardless of all the people around her who were being more negative. There are often people and situations around us which pose a real temptation to buy into negative cynicism or apathy.

However, we all can learn from Mary, to block out negative voices and to push them away—once we are convinced that we are doing the right thing. We can trust in our feelings and try to pursue what we believe is the right course of action. Whenever we get into complicated situations, we can be more open-minded, trusting that good things can come from things that initially seem negative or difficult.

Mary was so positive and full of hope—it's a great example to follow."

Eva-Maria Reiser

(Mary Magdalene in 2010)

"For me, Mary Magdalene was remarkable for the way in which she continued to trust in Jesus despite all the evidence to the contrary. She was a beacon of light, calling people around her to be positive and brave. In the Play, she was the one to speak words of hope to Jesus' mother, reminding her of Jesus' promises spoken in Bethany. She was an example of 'hope against hope.'

Playing this role for several months inevitably affects your everyday life. You can't just say, 'that's far away and totally irrelevant to my life!' There was a strange sense of power I experienced when 'back stage,' being able to help those who were still 'in role' and in a state of emotional grief through identifying with the biblical characters and all that they were going through. I found a strange 'power' to be myself a beacon of light, and I've tried to take this back into my normal life. When people ask me how I can be so positive, I have to say, 'I learnt it from Mary!'"

Jesus in the Upper Room & Gethsemane

THURSDAY (evening)

ACT IV: Jesus' Meal with His Disciples

From the dramatic and very public events in the temple, we move back once more to something private and intimate—Jesus having a meal with his disciples, the so-called "Last Supper."

For the many Jewish pilgrims who flocked to Jerusalem for the festival of Passover, everyone's goal was, if possible, to eat their Passover meal within the walls of the city. Jesus had evidently made some special prior arrangements with the owner of a house who had a guest room that would be large enough for Jesus and the Twelve. Almost certainly, it was a house somewhere in the southwestern quarter, known as the Upper City, where there were larger houses built for the wealthier members of the community. (It is possible, as has been argued elsewhere, that the house may indeed have belonged to the father of Mark, the later writer of Mark's Gospel; and also, that this was one of the places where the female followers of Jesus, such as his mother, had been staying the previous few nights).

But was this really a Passover meal? Many have noted that John's Gospel (13:1) strongly suggests that Jesus' crucifixion took place on the morning *before* the Passover feast began at sunset during the time when the lambs were being slaughtered in the temple prior to being cooked

Members of the 2010 Passion Play cast during the performance of the Last Supper scene

for the evening meal. Recent examination by astronomers into the lunar calendar in use around the year AD 30 has proved convincingly that John's chronology is correct, so we may need to conclude that Jesus was celebrating his own distinctive Passover meal *twenty-four hours ahead of schedule*. With hindsight, we now know why—twenty-four hours later he would be dead!

The disciples may have realized that Jesus was planning something slightly unusual and strictly irregular, but they were still in for a shock. First, Jesus insisted on washing their feet—something so embarrassing, that Peter fiercely objected. Then, midway through the special Passover liturgy (the *Haggadah*, with its recital of the original Passover events in Egypt), Jesus insisted that the ancient Israelites' "bread of affliction" was now to be understood as his own "body" and that the "cup of redemption" was his own "blood"—both things which all of them, as good Jews, would have seen as simply horrifying. After all, they never ate animal meat with

Living Image 4:
Hebrew Slaves under Egyptian Masters

Exodus 1:11-14; 2:23-24

They [the Egyptians] put slave masters over them [the Israelites] to oppress them with forced labor... They made their lives bitter;... in all their harsh labor the Egyptians worked them ruthlessly.... The Israelites groaned in their slavery... and God heard their groaning...

The experience of having once been slaves in Egypt marked the Jewish mindset for centuries to come. Each year at their Passover meal, they looked back to that time when the Egyptian pharaoh, threatened by this potential enemy within his territory, had resolved to oppress them—forcing them into slave labour. Yet miraculously, so they ardently believed, their God had on this occasion stepped in to rescue them—overpowering the oppressor, securing their escape, and eventually bringing them into a new home, the promised land.

That rescue is what Jesus' disciples would have been remembering and celebrating as they sat down to eat the Passover. Yet this was an ancient story with a modern ring. History had repeated itself, and they were once again experiencing political and economic oppression. This time they were not in exile in a strange land but were being oppressed by an absentee Roman emperor in their own homeland. All their fellow-Jews in Jerusalem would have echoed the complaint voiced in the days of Nehemiah: "we are slaves today, slaves in the land you gave our ancestors" (Nehemiah 9:36). They would have been praying earnestly that their God might once again hear their "groaning" and step in to rescue them from the hated Romans.

Looking back in later years on that last supper with Jesus, those same disciples would see it as the time in which their prayers were answered—but in a deeper and more mysterious way than they had ever envisaged. In Jesus, God had indeed been stepping into their world to rescue them—from evil in all its forms.

the blood still in it—for they had been taught that the blood represented the "life" that God had given (see Leviticus 17). They certainly were not cannibals eating human flesh! Jesus insisted that they ate and drank—"*all of you!*" Imagine the shock written on all their faces as they passed round the plate and then the cup.

From this scene, we can conclude that Jesus knew he was about to die, and he was actively intending to bring this down "upon his own head." Moreover, by evoking the Passover story, he was signaling that his imminent death would be looked back to as a divine act of rescue and deliverance on a par with the Exodus. Indeed, it would be an even greater Exodus. By saying those few words ("this is my body…; this is my blood") Jesus was self-consciously and deliberately placing himself in the great age-long sweep of the biblical story and saying that his death, not the Exodus, was its crowning moment: "do this in remembrance of *me*!" If one were then to dismiss the later claims in the Gospels for the resurrection of this Jesus from the dead, one would have to conclude that he had been a self-delusional fool. As for his followers, enjoying eating the body of their dead hero, they too should be promptly dismissed as sick and benighted. Why celebrate such a macabre meal?

Three days later, however, when the Gospel of Luke asserts that Jesus once again "broke bread" with his disciples on the Emmaus Road, things would begin to make sense. Right now, on this Thursday evening, the disciples must have felt that everything was shrouded in darkness and mystery. Jesus appeared to have a death wish. Why?

For Judas, this was the last straw. If Jesus was not going to be the kind of Messiah that Judas wanted Jesus to be—and, worse still, if he seemed already to be contemplating his own death—then this Jesus was worth abandoning to his self-inflicted fate. Judas leaves the room, heading for the nearby house of Caiaphas, the High Priest. In due course, the rest of the disciples leave too, heading down the steps from the Upper City towards the Siloam Gate. We read that they "sang a hymn," but one wonders who, if any, felt in the mood for singing quite now.

Jesus' praying on the Mount of Olives [during the 2010 Passion Play]

ACT V: Jesus on Mount of Olives—the Arrest

Gethsemane in Hebrew means "olive press." An olive press is precisely what one would expect to find at the foot of the Mount of Olives. In Jesus' day, it would probably have been a walled-off enclosure which during the day different farmers were allowed to use but which was suitably guarded at night. So, who let Jesus in?

One intriguing answer is that a young man, called Mark, had been told by his father to wait by the gate to let Jesus enter the enclosure as soon as he arrived. This concept then makes sense of a puzzling verse (found only in Mark's Gospel) which, later at the time of Jesus' arrest, refers to a "young man, wearing nothing but a linen garment" (effectively, just a night-shirt); when the men tried to seize him, "he fled naked, leaving his garment behind" (14:51-52). Almost certainly, this person is the author of the Gospel revealing this embarrassing moment: "I was there that night, but I ran away with absolutely nothing on!"

Jesus knew he would need some privacy, but privacy would be hard to find that night with thousands of Galilean pilgrims sleeping out all over the Mount of Olives. Hence his probable "double request" to Mark's

Living Image 5:
The Calling of Moses before the Burning Bush

Exodus 3:2-14

The angel of the LORD appeared to Moses in flames of fire from within a bush.

...Moses said, "Here I am."...

The LORD said, "I have indeed seen the misery of my people.... So I have come down to rescue them... So now, go. I am sending you to Pharaoh to bring my people the Israelites out of Egypt....

And God said I will be with you....

I AM WHO I AM.... say to the Israelites: 'I AM has sent me to you.'"

The episode of Moses' encounter with God in the burning bush was a key episode in the way the Hebrews told their story of the Exodus—their dramatic escape from Egypt. Their leader, despite his fears, had received a powerful new revelation from Israel's God: he was to be called by a new name ("I AM"). God was calling Moses to be the human being through whom God's rescue operation would be effected. Steeled by this vision and calling, Moses would go back to face the full wrath of Pharaoh—one man standing "solo" against a whole system of evil.

In the garden of Gethsemane, we see something similar: one man, alone, encountering God in prayer, and being steeled for a daunting mission as he heads back into the city into a veritable vortex of evil. Like Moses, Jesus effectively says, "Here I am; I am willing to go your way." Given what we see next—his steely resolve and determination—one can only conclude that Jesus had indeed received strength from the great I AM, receiving some assurance that his God would indeed achieve a victorious rescue—for Jesus himself and for his people. As the writer of Hebrews would later affirm: "during the days of Jesus' life on earth, he offered up prayers and petitions with fervent cries and tears to the one who could save him from death, and he was heard because of his reverent submission" (Hebrews 5:7).

Anton Burkhart
(Jesus in 2000)

"It was, of course, an incredible privilege to play the role of Jesus. As a dramatic part, it is quite a strange one because Jesus speaks so many words in the first half of the Play, but then is virtually silent throughout the second half. The role is obviously unique and different from other ones because of Jesus' unique value in the eyes of the audience. Few people really have a picture in their minds about, for example, Caiaphas or Pilate, but virtually everyone has a personal imagination of Jesus as a historical character. That means the actor playing Jesus may end up surprising or even disturbing those mental pictures. That's quite a scary feeling!

Back in the 1950s, Jesus was portrayed as though he were 'untouchable'—a divine figure who walked through the Play 'on a different level' to other mortals. In recent decades, there's been a deliberate attempt to work hard at showing him as a human being operating in complex situations (such as the temple) and for his image to be really well 'grounded' in historical reality— even if then the audience may wish to start rebuilding that image 'from the ground up.'

That made the scene in Gethsemane a particularly powerful one to enact. Jesus is on stage—almost alone—for a considerable amount of time, so it's very demanding. But instead of being tempted to play down the agony which Jesus went through, this focus on Jesus' true humanity gave me the encouragement to show Jesus going through a real crisis of confidence and entering into a very 'dark night of the soul.' He was fighting a very real battle, and his final 'not my will, but yours be done' only came about because of an agonizing time of wrestling in prayer.

Then there is the crucifixion scene. Up until 1990 Jesus was put up on the cross 'back stage.' In 2000, it was decided the audience should see Jesus actually being nailed to the cross and then strung up on high. I can remember at the first performance looking out from the cross and seeing the faces of the audience and the sheer look of horror on their faces. Of course, they knew that this was coming—it was no surprise—but they were deeply shocked by seeing the shameful treatment given to Jesus being enacted before their eyes. Yes, I felt the force of that shameful treatment myself—being 'on the receiving end' of it—but in many ways the audience seems to have felt its force even more.

So, was it a privilege to play the role of Jesus? Absolutely! As a Catholic myself, I do see the cross of Jesus as the 'way to God,' so taking on this role was very important to me and precious. I guess this meant I was able to play the part 'from the inside'—not as a detached observer but as a believer in the vital importance of Jesus' life and death. I'm not sure how my life might have been different if I had *not* played the role of Jesus, but playing that role certainly impacted my life deep down and, in many ways, confirmed me in my faith and in the way I want to live my life."

father—for use of the upper room for the Passover meal followed by access to his olive-press enclosure.

What time did Jesus reach Gethsemane? Perhaps, if he paused along the way, Jesus might have needed nearly an hour to get there from the Last Supper—walking out through the Siloam Gate and then up the floor of the Kedron Valley. We might suggest sometime around eleven o'clock.

And how long was he there? Given that fishermen are often well able to keep themselves awake all night, it's remarkable that Peter, James, and John fall asleep three times. The sleeping suggests the arresting party did not arrive until something like two o'clock in the morning.

What kept them so long? The answer, almost certainly, is that Caiaphas needed to make an urgent late-night visit to the Roman governor. The news that Judas brought—that Jesus seemed to be willing to give himself up and would be waiting in a quiet location through the night—had indeed been very welcome. It left things very tight for time. If they went out to arrest Jesus, they had to know that he would be dead before sunset the next day (the start of the Festival). If he was not (and they had to keep him in custody for the whole of Passover week), then the people would be in uproar.

The only solution was first to double-check with Pilate to see if he would agree to an emergency trial the next morning and would rubber-stamp their verdict. Caiaphas, we suggest, did indeed make that visit. (Some confirmation of this is found in Matthew 27:19 where we learn how Pilate's wife, Claudia Procula, had a bad dream about Jesus during the night—presumably because her husband had told her about Caiaphas' strange request before she went to sleep).

All this political maneuvering is going on in the city whilst Jesus prays and waits—for two or three hours. The fact that he waited for so long is yet another sign of his resolute determination to go the way of the cross. For, if he had wanted to, he could easily have walked up the Mount of Olives, and forty-five minutes later, have been settling into bed in the home of his friends in Bethany. How tempting that must have been! But Jesus chose neither to retreat nor to advance but simply to wait.

"*Abba*, Father," he said. . . . "Take this cup from me. Yet not what I will, but what you will" (Mark 14:36).

Here we see Jesus wrestling with God's will—longing with every sinew of his human body that there might be another way. Yet, it seemed there was none. In speaking about a *cup* (which picks up the imagery in the Hebrew prophets of the "cup of God's wrath" to be drunk by God's enemies), he revealed that during the coming day he would indeed be drinking this bitter "cup" down to its bottommost dregs. No wonder we read that he was in "'anguish'" and that his "sweat was like drops of blood falling to the ground" (Luke 22:44). Like the nearby olives that earlier that day had been crushed and "pressed"—not once but three times—in order to make the finest oil, Jesus was being squeezed and squeezed and squeezed again.

Frederik Mayet

(Jesus in 2010)

"Growing up in Oberammergau, there's inevitably lots of interest in who's going to be Jesus, so I was very excited when my name was announced for the 2010 season. That evening was so special! But the next morning, I suddenly felt overwhelmed with the pressure as I began to think: 'I so much respect the person of Jesus, how can I possibly play his part? And everyone has their own imagined picture of Jesus, how can I possibly fulfill their expectations? How can I bring Jesus alive on stage?!'

I was helped by watching a variety of other films about Jesus—like Franco Zeffirelli's *Jesus of Nazareth* or Mel Gibson's *The Passion of the Christ*. Each one gave me more insight into Jesus' character, but they also taught me that each portrayal of Jesus is *always an interpretation*. This realization meant I would need to develop my own interpretation to find *my own way of being Jesus*. No one else can do this for you. You have to feel it yourself.

My interpretation came together for me when, after months of rehearsals, we finally put on our costumes and had several weeks of dress rehearsals. Now at last, I could imagine myself really 'inhabiting' his character in a real way. Another key moment for me in rehearsals was when I was put up on the cross for the very first time. Obviously, the cross is very meaningful in our faith. But now, suddenly, *I was on that cross!* It was standing up vertically from the ground—and I was on it, half-naked, and experiencing the event's full brutality. At that moment, I felt I was at last getting closer to this person—going through the inside story of what he experienced.

Then there's the issue of trying to teach as Jesus taught. You have to mean every word you say. For example, in teaching the Lord's Prayer it was helpful that the script had a few tiny variations from the form used in church. I could not simply recite the words from memory, but I had to speak them out freshly as though I was teaching them for the first time!

In fact, the Play now has a greater amount of Jesus' teaching— including what he taught in Galilee. Without his teaching from Galilee, the impression can be given that Jesus simply came up to Jerusalem to die and that his death was not in any way the direct result of his having taught some very controversial things. Jesus was often speaking out on important topics, and it got him into trouble. In the Gospels, he's often speaking about social-justice issues, showing his heart for the poor, warning the rich, and including the outcasts. It's been good to weave in this material—it really makes Jesus' message seem relevant for our own day.

It's been a real honour to play the part of Jesus. Despite the obvious challenges, there's also a real sense that, in playing this role, you're not on your own; instead everybody in the village— both on stage and behind the stage—is working together with you. It's a community performance and a community experience. Yes, playing this role has also given me the opportunity to learn more about Jesus himself—both his character and his teaching. I'm not claiming it's made me a better person, but it has certainly changed my perspective on life. In particular, when I see how Jesus taught people so clearly but with such compassion, it's given me a greater confidence to try always to 'speak the truth in love.'"

At long last, Judas and the arresting party arrived. The waiting was over. Jesus gave himself up. After a brief scuffle, nine of the eleven disciples fled up the hill towards Bethany (where they probably stayed for the next seventy-two hours—fearful to come back into Jerusalem). Only Peter and John followed Jesus—but at a distance. When the main group of disciples looked back, they would have seen a few flaming torches going back towards the Upper City. Their master, they knew only too well, was about to be put on trial by Caiaphas, the High Priest.

Jesus in the House of Caiaphas

FRIDAY (before dawn)

ACT VI: Interrogations before Annas and the High Council

The high priest's residence would probably have been one of the largest and most sumptuous houses in the Upper City. Perhaps built on two floors, surrounding a central courtyard, it would have made for quite a contrast with the tiny homes that Jesus would have known so well from Nazareth and around Lake Galilee. The residence would have been very impressive and slightly intimidating.

Jesus would have arrived sometime between three and four in the morning. Not surprisingly, it seems that Caiaphas was still asleep—perhaps aiming to get a bare minimum of four hours' rest—and had asked his father-in-law, Annas, to interrogate the prisoner first on his behalf. Jesus gives little away in response, suggesting that Annas should ask all the people who have heard Jesus' teaching in public: "I said nothing in secret.... Ask those who heard me" (John 18:20-21).

Eventually Caiaphas arrives, as do some other members of the Jewish leading council, the Sanhedrin— some of whom may have been staying in the high priest's residence that night. Some try to stick false charges on Jesus. In particular, they try to work out his exact words when he had spoken of "destroying the temple." They recognize that Jesus is posing a

Model of Jerusalem at the time of Jesus showing the palace of Herod the Great (on the left) and other wealthy houses in the Upper City

threat to the temple of some kind—perhaps daring to set himself up as an alternative focus of worship for God's people—but they cannot get their evidence to agree.

At last Caiaphas asks Jesus outright: "Are you the Messiah, the Son of the Blessed One?" Asked a direct question, Jesus answers directly: "I am! And you will see the Son of Man sitting at the right hand of the Mighty One and coming on the clouds of heaven" (Mark 14:61-62).

At this time, Caiaphas tears his robes. He knows full well from the Hebrew Scriptures the implications of Jesus' few words. The "Son of Man" was an exalted figure who in the vision of the prophet Daniel had been portrayed as "coming with the clouds of heaven," approaching "the Ancient of Days," and then being ushered into the very presence of God—there to receive "authority" and "glory" from God, there to be worshiped by "all nations and peoples of every language," and to be given a kingdom that would "never be destroyed" (Daniel 7:13-14).

In the ears of Caiaphas such words are outrageous lunacy and evident signs of blasphemy. Who does Jesus think he is? Yet, they are also just the kind of words that Caiaphas had hoped might come out of Jesus' mouth.

Living Image 6:
The Prophet Daniel in the Lion´s Pit

Daniel 6:16, 19-22

…they brought Daniel and threw him into the lions' den.…

At the first light of dawn, the king got up and hurried to the lions' den.…he called to Daniel in an anguished voice, "Daniel, servant of the living God, has your God been able to rescue you from the lions?"

Daniel answered, "May the king live forever! My God…shut the mouths of the lions. They have not hurt me, because I was found innocent in his sight."

Throughout the biblical story, there would be times when solitary individuals—such as Joseph, Moses, or Jeremiah—had to stand up for their convictions and be ready to face the wrath of those with political power.

In this scene, we see a young man called Daniel, a courtier in the palace of King Darius, thrown into a den of lions because he has disobeyed a royal edict that all of the king's subjects should worship the king and no other god. Daniel's enemies find him pursuing his daily routine—praying by his open window three times a day to the God of Israel—and immediately report him to the king. By nightfall, Daniel has been sealed in a pit with several lions whilst the king—who personally favoured Daniel—has an anxious night wondering if Daniel's trust in God will vindicate him.

Jesus, standing before Annas and then Caiaphas, is following in Daniel's footsteps: one man, who a few hours earlier had been on his knees worshiping his God, has been denounced by his former colleagues, and now stands on trial. Will his innocence be vindicated? Will his trust in God, and his prayers, be answered? Or, if he is to be thrown into the ultimate pit of death, will his God somehow be able to rescue him from that dark place?

Living Image 7:
The Mocking of Job

Job 32:1-5

So these three men stopped answering Job.... But Elihu son of Barakel the Buzite...became very angry with Job...Elihu had waited before speaking to Job because they were older than he. But when he saw the three men had nothing more to say, his anger was aroused.

The Book of Job is a key part of the "Wisdom literature" within the Hebrew Bible. It offers an extended analysis of a key question asked by those who wish to believe in a God of love—why, if he exists and has power, do innocent people suffer in his world? Job is portrayed to the readers from the opening verse as genuinely innocent in God's sight—"blameless and upright, he feared God and shunned evil;" yet calamity is allowed to befall him—in part to see if his trust in God will stand the test.

Three of his friends (Eliphaz, Bildad, and Zophar) come to commiserate with him, but they each begin to remonstrate with him, arguing that he must be guilty—otherwise why would he be suffering so much? Thirty chapters later, young Elihu adds his fierce "righteous" anger—"rubbing salt" on Job's already festering wounds. Effectively, all four have put their friend on trial. They have mocked his protestations of innocence and thrown them back in his face.

So too, Jesus is now going through a mockery of a trial—his innocence being ridiculed. He will experience physical abuse and verbal mockery from soldiers. Perhaps even worse than these abuses, he will be betrayed by his friends. King David had reflected on this acute pain: "If an enemy were insulting me, / I could endure it... But it is you,...my close friend" (Psalm 55:12-13). Jesus is left utterly alone, bereft of companionship, entrusting himself entirely to his God. As his friend Peter would later conclude, "When they hurled insults at him, he did not retaliate...Instead, he entrusted himself to him who judges justly" (1 Peter 2:23).

For these words of blasphemy immediately cause those standing round to agree to a verdict that Jesus is "worthy of death." In the Hebrew Scriptures, a particular crime that deserved the death penalty was that of the false prophet who was leading Israel astray. Jesus evidently is just such a false prophet—in danger of corrupting the people of Israel.

Strictly, in Jewish law, trials at night-time were illegal. The Gospels clarify that, although Caiaphas' interrogation had probably started before dawn, there was a fuller and proper meeting of the "whole Sanhedrin" "very early in the morning" or "at daybreak"' (Mark 15:1; Luke 22:66). Bleary-eyed men arrive at the high priest's house to find that the prisoner has effectively already been condemned, but they now ratify that judgment with the necessary vote and then begin hurriedly to prepare their case for Jesus' next trial—this time before Pilate.

ACT VII: Jesus Is Mocked—Peter Denies Jesus—The Despair of Judas

Jesus is indeed experiencing "rough justice." There is little time for lengthy debate. Having arrested him at the dead of night, the authorities need to keep things moving. Jesus' case is passed from Annas to Caiaphas, from a small group in the high priest's house to a fuller meeting of the Sanhedrin, from there onto Pilate, onto Herod Antipas, and then back to Pilate—all in a matter of four or five hours.

Throughout that time, Jesus is the one person who has had no sleep but who has been awake and alert throughout the night—much of it spent in heart-wrenching prayer. As indicated by each of the four Gospels, he is also consistently on the receiving end of verbal mockery and physical abuse. We read how an official slaps Jesus in the face for speaking to the high priest in a way the official thought to be insolent; how those guarding Jesus blindfold him and then taunt him, saying "Prophesy! Who hit you?" (Luke 22:64); how later, Herod's soldiers will ridicule and mock him; and above all, how Pilate will order him to be flogged—not just *after* his sentencing but even *beforehand*. Evidently these were not trial

Living Image 8:
The Despair of Cain

Genesis 4:8-15

While they were in the field, Cain attacked his brother Abel and killed him....

The LORD said, "What have you done? Listen! Your brother's blood cries out to me....Now you are under a curse...You will be a restless wanderer on the earth."...Cain said to the LORD, "My punishment is more than I can bear.... I will be hidden from your presence...and whoever finds me will kill me."

But the LORD said to him, "Not so; anyone who kills Cain will suffer vengeance seven times over." Then the LORD put a mark on Cain so that no one who found him would kill him.

In the biblical account, Cain's killing of his brother, Abel, is portrayed as the first outworking of the Fall—a tragic insight into the hatred and evil that has entered into the human race, resulting in the murder even of one's own family members. It encapsulates the brokenness of our human condition and epitomizes "man's inhumanity to man."

We see this human brokenness breaking out throughout the Passion story: the cowardice of Peter, the treachery of Judas, the envy of the high priests, the political calculations of Pilate. This brokeness is the way we human beings operate: we all too easily play the role of Cain. So, as we watch those characters caught up in the drama of those Jerusalem events, we are not able to judge them— because in a profound sense, *they are us* and *we are them.*

Yet there is a surprising "twist" at the end: God places a mark of protection on Cain the murderer. This speaks loudly of God's grace and forgiveness towards sinful human beings. And we see that being demonstrated in Jesus. Though denied by Peter, betrayed by Judas and vilified by the various rulers, Jesus seemingly absorbs all this "inhumanity to man," taking the full brunt of it "on the chin." He is demonstrating another way of being human—overcoming the force of hatred and evil with the greater power of ever-forgiving love.

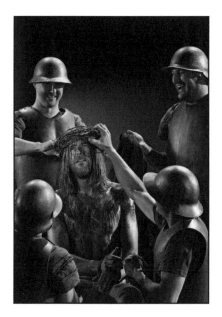

A scene from the 2010 Passion Play in which the Roman soldiers place a crown of thorns on Jesus' head to mock the idea of him as a king

proceedings where the defendant might expect justice to be administered impartially.

The Roman soldiers will fulfill this command—making things worse by putting a purple robe on him, placing a crown of thorns on his head and paying mock homage to him as a supposed "king of the Jews."

It's not impossible that Jesus received the traditional Jewish punishment of thirty-nine lashes (something which the apostle Paul would later claim to have received no less than *five* times, see 2 Corinthians 11:24). However, the time constraints of those few hours may have meant Jesus did not receive the full force of the law in this way. That punishment may have been left to the Roman authorities.

Whatever the precise details, we are seeing here the worst of man's inhumanity to man. What is being exposed here is not the wrong-doing of the Jewish or Roman guards on that particular day but, more deeply, the dark material of all our human hearts. It is our tendency as human beings to exploit and demean those under our power, abusing their persons, and denying their human dignity—the precise opposite of what Jesus himself had taught with his catch-phrase "do to others what you would have them do to you" (Matthew 7:12). Jesus is indeed experiencing the full brunt of human sin and evil in some of its ugliest manifestations.

* * * * *

Anton Burkhart

(Caiaphas in 2010)

"In the 1950s, Caiaphas' role was by far the biggest one in the Play. He was on stage in so many scenes, and he certainly had the most words to deliver. In recent decades, however, this has changed. We knew we needed to avoid the simplistic caricature of Caiaphas as the bad Jewish leader being contrasted with Pilate portrayed as the good Roman leader. So now the focus is more on Caiaphas as a political leader who is struggling to hold together a fragile peace with the Romans whilst Pilate is seen for the malevolent ruler that we know from Josephus that he truly was.

This change made playing Caiaphas' part far more interesting. I started thinking myself into Jerusalem's complicated politics with various Jewish groups jostling for power. There was a significant clash between the Sadducees, such as the high priest's family, and the Zealots who responded to the Romans with quite opposite strategies. Sadducees, like Caiaphas, wanted to keep the status quo and not rock the boat, whilst the Zealots, including people like Barabbas, wanted to fight the pagan oppressor and achieve Jewish independence.

I began to see things (even if I did not agree with him) from Caiaphas' point of view. After years of developing a delicately balanced way of cooperating with the Romans, he was now confronted in Jesus with a Messianic claimant who singlehandedly might blow everything apart!

I found myself thinking of modern political situations—such as in the Middle East or Afghanistan—where local religious leaders need to work out how they can cooperate and get along with the region's dominant military power. It's not easy, and you may go to quite extreme lengths to keep the peace. After all, in such tense political situations, it doesn't take much of a spark to set the whole region ablaze with further bloodshed.

This understanding then makes sense of the statement on Caiaphas' lips in John's Gospel, when he concludes that it is better 'that one man [Jesus] die for the people than that the whole nation perish' (John 11:50). The Sanhedrin were evidently concerned that Jesus might develop a popular following which might then attract the attention of the Romans who in response might then 'come and take away both our temple and our nation' (v. 48). Faced with *that* alternative, Caiaphas' cruel calculation—that only one person needs to die, not thousands—made some kind of sense.

I also wondered if Caiaphas viewed Jesus with some snobbery—not talking to Jesus because he was a nobody compared to himself who came from a very respectable lineage of high priests. Perhaps, instead, he was slightly afraid. Maybe it was a combination of the two?!

In 2020, I will instead be playing Joseph of Arimathea. Again, in the light of the wrong caricature of all the Jewish leaders being opposed to Jesus, I'm sure we will be showing that there were a good number of Jewish leaders, such as Joseph, who were speaking up on Jesus' behalf and disagreeing with Caiaphas' 'expedient' solution. I'm looking forward to seeing how Caiaphas and Pilate respond!"

There are also other human weaknesses being exposed that night—the failed bravado of Peter and the confused remorse of Judas. Each one of us, we soon realize, could have found ourselves in either of those roles on that night:

- In the story of what Judas did, we see an example of how we too can turn against our friends. We can be so offended that others do not fall in line with our preferred agendas that we become angry with them and sacrifice them on the altar of our own plans. We can be tempted by promises of money or favour to abandon our own integrity.
- Similarly, in the story of what Peter did, we see an example of how we too can be falsely confident of own strength and resolve. We can

assume that the only way to achieve things in life is to "fight our corner." We can make fine-sounding promises but fail to deliver.

Viewing the Passion story in this light, we can then take encouragement from a key sentence contained in Luke's account. Just after Peter has denied any knowledge of Jesus for the third time, we read:

> Just as he was speaking, the rooster crowed. The Lord turned and looked straight at Peter. Then Peter remembered the word the Lord had spoken to him: "Before the rooster crows today, you will disown me three times." And he went outside and wept bitterly.
>
> *(Luke 22:60-62)*

Jesus "looked straight at Peter." This statement is perfectly feasible from a historical point of view. For example, Jesus might well have been standing on a balcony and thus have been able to look down into the courtyard and catch Peter's eye.

One can only imagine what Peter felt at that moment—looking into the eye of Jesus, his friend and master. He knew his failings had been fully exposed. Yet—from all that we know of Jesus, both in the Gospels and the rest of the New Testament—we may also surmise that Jesus' eyes were communicating not dismissive judgment but kindness and understanding. Right now, Peter might not be able to make any sense of it. Yet in the coming weeks, this same Jesus would give him opportunities to know his continuing love—despite his so evident failings.

Encountering the knowing eyes of Jesus brought healing and forgiveness to Peter—something which, if the fundamental message of the New Testament is to be received, can also become a reality for everyone. This forgiveness then gave Peter the confidence some thirty years later, as he continued to ponder the significance of that night's traumatic events and their implications for people all around the world, to write about Jesus in his role as a good "shepherd" who can bring forgiveness to any wayward sheep:

*When they hurled their insults at him, he did not retaliate;
when he suffered, he made no threats. Instead, he entrusted
himself to him who judges justly. "He himself bore our sins" in
his body on the cross... "by his wounds you have been healed."
For "you were like sheep going astray," but now you have
returned to the Shepherd and Overseer of your souls.*

(1 Peter 2:23-25)

Carsten Lück
(Judas in 2000 & 2010)

Anton (Toni) Preisinger
(Judas in 2000)

"There are obviously some real challenges in playing Judas. In older versions of the Play, he was the story's principal 'bad guy'—along with Caiaphas. Apparently, in the 1920s after the end of the performance, the actor playing Judas might sometimes be spat upon by members of the audience who despised Judas for his treachery towards Jesus. We never received that ourselves, but we knew when we accepted the role that it was going to be tough.

The single toughest thing turned out to be the long scene in which Judas commits suicide. You're solo on stage for over fifteen minutes, and it's really demanding—both physically and mentally. All eyes are on you, and you need to get yourself fully immersed in Judas' own mindset—to sense his confusion and then desperation, to feel it 'from the inside.' He was in a real dilemma. You need to feel his struggling and his mental turmoil.

From the year 2000 onwards, the director wanted Judas' role to be portrayed in new ways. In particular, he wanted us to show—both in some revised script and also in our body-language on stage—that Judas and Jesus had been good friends. There was some real warmth and respect between them. Judas wasn't always on the outside of the group—as it were, acting as a spy from the outset. No, only in the last few days did Judas change his mind.

Judas' reasons for doing so were not just about money. Yes, he may have been in charge of the money-bag at the time of Mary's anointing Jesus in Bethany and sometimes a thief (according to John 12:6), but his betraying Jesus is unlikely to have been simply for greed. After all, within that first-century world the 'thirty pieces of silver' was only the amount needed in order to redeem a slave—not a vast sum of money. Judas initially shows no interest in receiving any money at all and eventually only receives it reluctantly.

Instead we developed the idea—in keeping with what we know of the complex political situation at the time—that Judas' motives for betraying Jesus may well have been more political. Like many Zealots, he probably wanted Jesus to confront the Romans head-on. After all, if he was really the Messiah, then surely that was what one would expect! So, when Jesus began to reveal that was not his intention, Judas was bitterly disappointed. It's possible even that, in going down the route of betraying Jesus, Judas was actually trying to force Jesus' hand—provoking him into the action that Judas thought was now required.

All this complexity helps to redeem Judas' role from the too-easily-adopted stereotypes. He was a real human being who found himself immersed in a very difficult situation where the best way forward was not clear. That, of course, doesn't suddenly make his actions right, but at least it makes them understandable—enough perhaps to evoke in us all some elements of real sympathy."

Jesus before the Authorities

FRIDAY (early morning)

ACT VIII: Jesus before Pilate and Herod

For a long time now, it has been assumed that Jesus would have been presented for trial before Pontius Pilate in the Roman army barracks just to the north of the temple. This Antonia Fortress (named in honour of Mark Anthony) would have housed hundreds of Roman soldiers who were deployed to keep the awkward peace in the temple precincts and elsewhere. It would be a very safe place for Pilate to stay during those few times each year when he needed to visit this turbulent city.

Yet there was another option—one which may have appealed somewhat more to his wife—the luxurious palace that the now-deceased Herod the Great had built some 40 years earlier. This site was equally secure and had the added advantage of being located just inside the city's western walls and having its own private gate. Thus, Pilate's entourage could get into Jerusalem without having to risk going through any of its streets.

Modern archaeologists believe they have recently found evidence for this gate and can now suggest what that scene may have looked like on that Friday morning. The religious leaders (not wanting to defile themselves for the Passover by entering properly into the governor's pagan palace) may well have come through that gate and into an inner gatehouse courtyard where they could remain at the foot of some stairs to the left which proceeded up to the governor's palace (or "*Praetorium*"). The platform at the top of the stairs should thus probably be identified with the place mentioned in John's Gospel (19:13) called *Gabbatha*, an Aramaic word for a "Stone Pavement." This platform would be the location for Pilate's judgment seat. From here, Pilate could easily take Jesus away for a private conversation in a nearby room—something which we see him doing at least twice (John 18:33-38; 19:8-12).

If this is correct, then we may be able to get a closer estimate on the numbers in the crowd on that day. Space in such a gatehouse courtyard would have been strictly limited. Even if all seventy members of the Sanhedrin council came *en masse*, how many ordinary people would have joined them? Especially, we might add, so early on this important day of Passover preparation? After all, many men, as leaders of their Jewish household, would have been busy collecting their lambs from the temple for their evening meal.

Given too that the authorities were fearful of the masses, fearing they might riot when they heard what had happened to Jesus, they would want as few people as possible becoming aware of what they were up to. Perhaps they cajoled a few "miscreants" to join them, who they could rely on to support their cause, but the total number is most unlikely to have exceeded a hundred—conceivably significantly less. This crowd is thus a very different crowd to the one which welcomed Jesus a few days earlier. There is no way that the actions of this tiny group—despite many horrid anti-Semitic accusations in subsequent centuries—can somehow be then applied *en masse* to a whole people-group.

Whatever the case, Jesus is brought before Pilate perhaps around seven o'clock or soon after. Pilate asks what Jesus is officially charged with (formerly known in Latin as the *accusatio*) and is told: "We have found this man subverting our nation" (in other words, he is a false prophet "leading Israel astray"). Yet they know this religious *accusatio* on its own may not stick with Pilate. They continue in a more political direction: "He opposes payment of taxes to Caesar (which readers of the Gospels know is a downright lie) and he claims to be Messiah, a king" (Luke 23:2). Now *that* should cause Pilate some concern!

Pilate then asks Jesus privately about his supposed "kingdom" (John 18:33-37) but soon returns to the platform, convinced in his own mind that Jesus is not any kind of king about which he or his bosses in Rome need to be too troubled. Jesus' accusers then mention that he first started

Exodus 12:29-31

At midnight the LORD struck down all the firstborn in Egypt, from the firstborn of Pharaoh, who sat on the throne, to the firstborn of the prisoner... there was loud wailing in Egypt.... Pharaoh summoned Moses and Aaron and said, "Up! Leave my people, you and the Israelites! Go!"

Moses had stood many times before Pharaoh, the omnipotent potentate who ruled the world of that time, and had continually demanded the release of the Hebrews. He was one seemingly insignificant individual, standing alone against an entire system. What hope could he have in such a beleaguered situation? But then the "passing over" of God's judgment intervened, causing Pharaoh, who many times had prevaricated, to change his mind.

Jesus now stands before Pilate and Herod—those with all the political power in the world of his day. Again, it's one solitary man standing against an entire system of worldly power, and again, it's Passover season and God's people are longing for freedom from the pagan oppressor. Is there any hope?

Pilate prevaricates. He is trying to work out what to do with Jesus and what will best serve his selfish purposes, but eventually he dismisses Jesus to be crucified. Brute force, oppressive political power, has seemingly had the last word. Apparently, "might is right" and the hopes of longed-for freedom are evidently built on sand.

Yet, there is a twist. Three days later, so the Gospel writers assert, divine power revisits the world, bringing an even deeper rescue. A new Passover has been accomplished—bringing vindication for Jesus and for all who long for freedom from the oppressive power of evil itself. It turns out that Pilate, like Pharaoh before him, who has embodied many of the worst aspects of human power and evil, has been outmaneuvered by an even greater power, full of goodness and truth.

stirring up this trouble in Galilee. This accusation immediately gives Pilate the get-out clause for which he was beginning to hope. He promptly sends Jesus off to be tried instead by Herod Antipas (the son of Herod the Great who, more than 30 years after his father's death, still ruled over the region of Galilee).

Herod may well have been staying in the Hasmonean Palace, named after the dynasty that had ruled over Judea during a century of Jewish independence (167-67 BC). This palace was quite nearby, so twenty minutes or so later, Jesus stands on trial yet again.

This Herod was the one who had ordered John the Baptist's execution and who, when he heard about Jesus' increased popularity in Galilee, began even to wonder if John was somehow "back from the dead" (see Matthew 14:2). This Herod too had let it be known that he wanted to kill Jesus; Jesus sent his reply to this threat, addressing Herod as a wily "fox" (Luke 13:31-32).

Jesus was not going to get a fair trial here either. In fact, after plying him with questions, Herod seems more interested in getting Jesus to perform a stunt miracle for him; and then, when that does not materialize, simply instructs his soldiers to ridicule and mock Jesus. Herod's prime goal is not any quest for truth and justice but rather for frivolity and laughter. In every sense of the word, this proceeding is a mockery of a trial.

ACT IX: Jesus Condemned by Pilate

Jesus' trial must rank as the most contorted scene described in the Gospels: plot and counterplot, accusations and rejoinders, blame-shifting amongst Jesus' accusers, shouting and rabble-rousing, political machinations, and religious rancour—it's all going on around Jesus as he stands there, calmly and knowingly, in its midst.

At this distance in time, the task of reconstructing a coherent sequence of events is obviously impossible—even though the Gospels have given us a good idea of the main issues that were voiced that morning. After all,

Living Image 10:
Joseph Interprets Pharaoh's Dream

Psalm 105:16-21

[God] called down famine on the land /…and sent a man before them— / Joseph, sold as a slave. / They bruised his feet with shackles, /…till what he foretold came to pass, /… The king sent and released him, /…and made him…/ ruler over all he possessed.

The story of Joseph (told as a 'saga' in Genesis 37-50) is a vital backstory standing behind the story of the Exodus under Moses.

This young teenager, despised by his older brothers as an arrogant dreamer, is sold by them into slavery and transported off to Egypt where he soon finds himself unjustly thrown into prison. In that dark place, he yet establishes his reputation as one able to interpret dreams and is eventually brought into the royal palace. Pharaoh has had two similar dreams (about cows and about heads of grain) which Joseph now sees as a prophecy of seven years of plentiful harvests to be followed by seven years of severe famine. He is duly honoured by Pharaoh as his chief of staff—charged with the task of managing Egypt's food supply.

After many years of ignominy, this moment is the time of Joseph's vindication. It is also the moment when Joseph is established in the position from which he will later act as the rescuer of his brothers—preventing them from starving to death due to the extreme famine. At the saga's conclusion, we will hear Joseph speaking words of forgiveness to his brothers, "you intended to harm me, but God intended it for good to accomplish what is now being done, the saving of many lives" (Genesis 50:20). Their act of hatred turns out to be the means of their salvation.

Setting this powerful paradigm—of divine providence working through human evil—behind the story of Jesus helps us see it with new eyes. Jesus, condemned by Pilate, is seemingly being rejected by humanity as a whole, but is he also being placed in the position from which he can soon act as humanity's rescuer?

Pilate's condemning of Jesus to death [during the 2010 Passion play]

particular arguments may well have "gone round in circles" or been picked up by different sections of the crowd at different times.

- Mark's account is the shortest and indeed is so brief (containing just five quick questions from Pilate) that, if this were received as a comprehensive account, the trial would have lasted less than two minutes!

- Matthew has used Mark's account as his template but has then added the information about Pilate's wife's dream and his hand-washing.

- Luke gives a slightly different account. He alone mentions Jesus' trial before Herod Antipas and specifies that Pilate declared Jesus' innocence three times.

- John's account is the longest, including private conversations between Pilate and Jesus as well as more precise details about the time and place—all of which may suggest that this is eyewitness testimony from Jesus' disciple, John (the only male disciple to witness Jesus' trial and execution).

There is indeed complexity in these accounts. This complexity does not require historians to be dismissive towards them, but rather to value their different perspectives which, taken together, allow us a much greater access to the original event than we would otherwise have.

The overall picture is clear. The Gospel writers are convinced that Jesus had been innocent of all the political charges levied against him. If he was the Messiah (as, of course, they strongly affirmed), he was a quite different Messiah from someone like Barabbas who was a political insurrectionist against Rome. In fact, that nationalistic agenda was precisely what Jesus had warned people to avoid. Yet, here before Pilate, in a deep irony, he had ended up taking Barabbas' place and being condemned to die on a cross—the punishment that the Romans meted out expressly for political rebels. Paradoxically—and precisely because of his profound love for his own Jewish fellow-countrymen—Jesus would never *speak* in favour of the cause of Jewish nationalism, but he would end up *dying* for it.

This confusion as to the precise nature of Jesus' Messiahship explains much of the crisscross machinations that were played out that day. The general populace longed for a nationalistic Messiah. However, Caiaphas and many of the Sanhedrin were Sadducees who tried to suppress this nationalistic ardour and curried favour with the Roman authorities (whose presence they yet still fiercely hated). When Jesus revealed to Caiaphas that he saw himself as the exalted "Son of Man" (a mysterious personage presumed to be far *greater* than a mere *human* "Messiah"), this placed the Sanhedrin in a paradoxical situation. This prisoner was *not*, after all, guilty of being the "political" type of "Messiah" that they feared; but he *was* guilty (unless, of course, he was correct—which, from their perspective, was absurd) of having exalted notions about himself as someone worthy of worship—which was utter blasphemy.

Under Jewish law, blasphemy required the death penalty. Since AD 6 the Sanhedrin had lost the right to execute people, so they would have to take this prisoner to the Roman authorities for sentencing. Under Roman

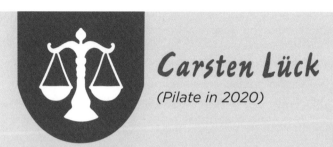

Carsten Lück
(Pilate in 2020)

"Well, after playing the role of Judas, I now have the opportunity to act as the *real* villain in the piece!

Over the years, we've begun to see what a monster this man, Pilate, was. I've found it particularly interesting to hear what the ancient Jewish historian Josephus had to say about this infamous procurator of Judea.

- He was constantly provoking the Jewish leaders by doing things they found deeply offensive. He was certainly not afraid to 'kick up a storm' even if it caused howling protests.
- He was ruthless in enforcing his authority. Apparently, a few years later, even the Romans were appalled by his brutality in putting down a Samaritan rebellion, so they brought him back to Rome to explain his actions!

So, I'm going to have no hesitation in portraying him as an evil character—intent on only one thing, preserving his power and authority.

I don't know what it says about me, but there have been other plays where I've been cast as a strong leader. For example, I played the title character in *Moses* (written by Feridun Zaimoglu and Günter Senkel, directed by Christian Stückl). I know that in some situations strong leadership is indeed a good thing and something which human societies need. Yet, there is a massive difference between good and bad leadership, between the good use of power and its complete abuse. It's this evil, totalitarian, abuse of power that we see in Pilate—something which, sadly, we also see in our own contemporary world.

I realize that for the Gospel writers their supreme concern is to show that Jesus was innocent. They have to explain to their readers how the one they follow has ended up dead on a Roman cross. After all, that would normally mean the crucified person was a criminal—not the supposed 'Saviour of the world!' Yet in getting Pilate—no less than three times—to declare that Jesus is innocent, they perhaps unwittingly give the impression that Pilate too was fairly innocent.

In fact, the principal reason why Pilate eventually 'washed his hands' was instead—as the Gospel writers make quite clear—because he was caught in an awkward political *impasse*. If he was lenient to a person like Jesus who claimed to be a Jewish 'king', then his boss in Rome, the emperor, could easily accuse him of treason. 'If you let this man go, you are no friend of Caesar' (John 19:12). Faced with such a challenge, Pilate had no hesitation in preserving his own life and discarding Jesus' life.

I think we will be portraying Pilate this year as the one who must take the fullest responsibility for the death of Jesus. This was *his* decision to make, and *he* was the one who made it."

law, blasphemy was not a crime. What *would* be criminal in their eyes was anyone claiming to be a political Messiah! Hence the Sanhedrin's attempts to hoist onto Jesus the charge of being such a political Messiah—even though they probably knew, deep down, *this was what Jesus was not*.

The Gospel writers indicate that Pilate saw through this machination, detecting that Jesus was no ordinary "Messiah" or "King" and instead surmised that part of what was driving the Sanhedrin's determination was "envy" or "self-interest" (Mark 14:9). Yet, they then show him refusing to do the right thing—using delaying tactics and other strategies rather than letting Jesus go free. Note how, even if in his eyes Jesus is innocent of the particular charge levied against him, Pilate still callously suggests that Jesus should first be punished (Luke 23:16) and has him flogged during the middle of the trial (John 19:1-3). Pilate is thereby revealed as no lover of justice and one given to the brutal abuse of his power. In fact, in AD 36 this man's savage butchery in response to a revolt amongst the Samaritans would be so shocking to the Roman emperor (even Caligula) that he was deposed from office and ordered back to Rome. The very "Caesar" whom he was fearful of offending now by releasing Jesus would, a few years later, dismiss him instead for crucifying hundreds of Samaritans.

No one in this drama around Jesus emerges with honour or integrity. Everyone is tainted with self-interest and dishonesty. Everyone is seen playing games and passing the buck. Jesus is surrounded by human evil in all its forms.

What we are seeing here—on the stage of this court scene—is a graphic portrait writ large of our own human nature: the worst of us, that often lies buried in our own hearts, now bursts forth like a volcano—emblazoned for all to see. This nature means that the ultimate lesson can never be that we start wagging our fingers self-righteously at individual characters or groups played out in this scene—piling the blame onto them. Instead, those fingers need to be pointed back at ourselves. What I am seeing in this drama is what I pretend away and normally refuse to see—myself. As the saying goes, "there, but for the grace of God, go I."

Jesus at Golgotha

FRIDAY (middle day)

ACT X: The Way of the Cross—Crucifixion

Jesus is led out from Pilate's *Praetorium* towards a place of execution—known in Aramaic as *Golgotha* (the "place of the skull," later translated into Latin as *Calvary*). The precise location of these two sites has been hotly debated over the years. However, if as argued previously, Pilate was staying that weekend in the palace of the former King Herod the Great, and if the traditional site of Golgotha (being now marked by the church of the Holy Sepulchre) is accepted, then the distance involved would have been only a few hundred yards. (For fuller arguments, see my books

Jesus's carrying of his cross along the Via Dolorosa [during the 2010 Passion Play]

The Weekend that Changed the World and *In the Steps of Jesus*.) Jesus goes out through what Josephus later called Jerusalem's "second wall," using the *Gennath* (or "Garden") Gate, and soon is brought to a disused quarry [an area of about 50 yards square].

Many years earlier, the stonemasons had left this area to go wild, so the bare rocks had been gradually covered with soil. Some rough vegetation and wild flowers had then grown up, creating a kind of garden area in some parts of the quarry. The stonemasons had also left a small outcrop of rock [about 15 feet high and 20 feet in diameter) freestanding in the midst of the quarry—almost certainly because its limestone rock was cracked and useless for building blocks. This small knoll (or hillock) may conceivably have looked like a human skull, giving rise to the name *Golgotha*; however, that name may instead have come about simply because this whole quarry was frequently used as a place of execution.

In any event, this area of Golgotha was a convenient place. The Romans liked their crucifixions to be enacted close to main roads, so that passersby could get the message of what happened to political rebels.

Genesis 22:16-18

"I swear by myself, declares the LORD, that because you...have not withheld your son, your only son, I will bless you and make your descendants as numerous as the stars...through your offspring all nations on earth will be blessed, because you have obeyed me."

This divine promise is given to Abraham after he had felt God's call to offer his only son, Isaac, as a sacrifice and had proceeded to bind Isaac on an altar—only then to hear God's call to stop. Looking up, Abraham suddenly saw nearby a ram, caught by its horns in a thicket. The ram took Isaac's place. And Abraham—no doubt mightily relieved at this last-minute reprieve—named that place, "the LORD will provide" (Genesis 22:14).

This episode has long been pondered in both the Jewish and Christian traditions for its deeper significance. At a superficial level, it is strange: God seemingly proposes a child-sacrifice— something which later Hebrew prophets denounce as "detestable" in his sight (see Ezekiel 23:36-37).

The first Christians, looking back on Jesus' crucifixion, soon began to see in it a powerful advanced picture of the Cross. In some ways Abraham, they reflected, was doing what Jesus himself did— pursuing a path of determined obedience and trusting in God's ultimate provision. In other ways, Abraham was even enacting the role of God himself by being ready to offer as a sacrifice the most precious thing in his sight—his only Son. Hence Paul's words when describing God's grace: "He who did not spare his own Son, but gave him up for us all" (Romans 8:32). Seen in this light, Jesus' crucifixion, despite its horror at one level, can be seen more deeply as an act of deep love—God graciously providing the very sacrifice he had appointed and giving for us his most precious gift.

Hence, the reference in Mark's Gospel (15:21) to an African man, Simon of Cyrene, who was forced to carry Jesus' cross-beam (or *patibulum*) simply because he was "passing by on his way in from the country." Many Passover visitors and many local shoppers going about their daily business—some perhaps carrying their water jars fresh from the cisterns cut underneath one side of the quarry—will have seen the grisly scene. Amongst them were Jesus' own friends: the disciple John, Jesus' mother, and a good number of Jesus' female followers.

Traditionally, it has been imagined that Jesus, together with two other brigands, was crucified on the top of a hill. Yet, the Gospels never mention a "hill" (simply referring to the "place" of Golgotha). Quite possibly, these crucifixions (which required some space between them) took place on the floor of the quarry—whether near the base of the small hill or even forty yards away on the other side of the quarry.

"And they crucified him" (Mark 15:24). Mark's account is matter-of-fact. In just fifteen verses, he mentions the *titulus* ("the King of the Jews"), the sneering comments of passersby, the strange darkness at midday, Jesus' quotation from Psalm 22:1 ("My God, my god, why have you forsaken me?"), and the Roman centurion's final declaration from Mark 15:39 ("Surely this man was the Son of God!").

Despite all that this scene must have meant to the first followers of Jesus, Mark's account does not betray those emotions or develop the *pathos* of the scene, nor is there any comment on its ugly brutality. Even the fact that Jesus was almost certainly hanging on the cross completely naked (something so shameful in a Jewish culture) is only hinted at in Mark's reference to the soldiers casting lots for his clothes.

The other Gospel writers are similarly restrained. Matthew adds a reference to an earthquake at the moment of Jesus' death. Luke portrays a conversation between Jesus and one of the others being crucified. It is left to John to add some editorial comments and to include a little more emotional colour—in particular, describing that precious moment when

John 3:14-16

"Just as Moses lifted up the snake in the wilderness, so the Son of Man must be lifted up, that everyone who believes may have eternal life in him.

For God so loved the world that he gave his one and only Son, that whoever believes in him shall not perish but have eternal life."

In his conversation with Nicodemus, Jesus had gently chided this teacher of Israel for not understanding various heavenly things which he, Jesus, as the Son of Man was trying to teach Nicodemus. One was about this strange future event when Jesus would in some way be lifted up. What did he mean?

Later in John's Gospel, Jesus would use this phrase again, "when I am lifted up from the earth, [I] will draw all people to myself." John adds, "he said this to show the kind of death he was going to die" (John 12:32-33). For John the moment of Jesus' being "lifted up" is evidently his imminent crucifixion.

This phrase has two, very different, backgrounds in the Hebrew Scriptures. One, as Jesus told Nicodemus, is Moses' lifting up a bronze snake in the desert. The Israelites, experiencing a time of judgment because of their disobedience, had been urged to look up from their suffering to what God was lifting up for them as a means of rescue. "Look at my crucifixion," Jesus effectively is teaching, "and you will find it a place of healing and rescue."

The other is found in the prophecies of Isaiah: in an opening vision (6:1) Isaiah sees the Lord "high and exalted" and then in a later one (52:13) he sees God's servant being "lifted up and highly exalted." Based on this second theme, John understands Jesus' being "lifted up," despite its shame and indignity, as a place of God's exalted glory.

On the day of the Crucifixion, John may have seen only tragedy and disgrace, but with hindsight and guided by these biblical insights, he came to see it as the revelation of God's loving rescue and dazzling glory.

Helga Stuckenberger

(Mary Magdalene in 1984, 1990, and 2000)

"It was an incredible privilege to play the part of Mary Magdalene not once but three times. I have been on stage each year in some role or other—as one of the children in 1970, as Veronica in 1980, as Martha in 2010—and I look forward in the 2020 season to being one of the 'daughters of Jerusalem' weeping for Jesus on his way to the cross. There was something very special about being Mary Magdalene and doing so three times certainly gave me the opportunity to grow into the role.

Mary has an intuitive understanding of who Jesus is and what he's come to do. The male disciples—perhaps using their very best rational faculties—cannot see this. Mary is in touch with her heart. She has a heart-to-heart relationship with Jesus. We see something of this in the Gospels, when we hear Jesus commending her for her anointing him: 'She has done a beautiful thing to me...she did what she could' (Mark 14:6-8). That's the language of the heart, and we see it in the Play. Later, on the way to the cross when Mary speaks to Jesus, 'My heart breaks; your heart breaks!'

Between 1984 and 2000, we began to express more of this in the Bethany anointing scene. In 1990, we introduced the idea of Mary anointing Jesus as a king, and then in 2000, her anointing him as an act of love. When Mary longed to go with Jesus to Jerusalem but he said 'No', there was a new dialogue (based on the Old Testament book, the Song of Songs) in which Jesus spoke as a bridegroom to his 'beloved.' In this way, Mary took on the role of God's people, Israel, waiting longingly for the Messiah's coming. It was a beautiful way of picking up the Bible's male/female imagery in a way that was not sexual but which deeply honoured Mary's female love for Jesus. She was responding as a woman to God's love which she could sense in the person of

Jesus. That speaks of a powerful reality today—namely that the Lord has indeed given us all this ability to feel and to understand.

Of course, Mary Magdalene is the one who has the 'punch line' of the entire story. She's the first to proclaim the Resurrection! It was always quite a challenge as an actor to make the transition from Mary being in a state of panic and disbelief to her suddenly being in a place of joy and wonder. In 2000, the message of the Resurrection was brought to Mary, not through the risen Jesus himself, but rather through an angel. In some ways, that made the transition even more difficult to portray. The change was now something more clearly *within* Mary's own way of thinking not simply brought about by something *outside* her, based on having herself seen Jesus. I think this way of presenting Mary actually had the good effect of making Mary's testimony seem more reliable and trustworthy. It was not just an 'idle tale' easily dismissed by the apostles, but it was something which showed her own powerful ways of thinking and reasoning.

From my early teenage years, I can remember the excitement of attending the early morning service at five o'clock on Easter Day and being there to welcome the risen Jesus. That time was long before I knew I might play the part of Mary Magdalene, so there's a sense in which this role has always been part of my life. At the end of the day, I have to say, 'I am Helga, but it's also true that this person, Mary, is somehow a part of me—indeed *in* me!'"

Jesus said goodbye to his mother, entrusting her in her inconsolable grief to the care of John.

Jesus would have been hanging on the cross for two or three hours, writhing in agony; and, throughout that time, Jesus' followers would have been watching him slowly dying. Words simply fail to describe the agonies of those hours. To see a friend die in such painful and shameful circumstances would be bad enough. How much worse when that friend had spoken such truth, had used his powers to do such good, had spoken of his God with so much faith, and had caused you to pin your own faith and hope on him? Now the embodiment of that truth and goodness was slowly being extinguished and that faith and hope was slowly being buried before your eyes.

Eventually, Jesus himself was buried. Taken down from the cross, he was given some preliminary embalming by Nicodemus and Joseph of Arimathea. They had to act quickly—sunset was approaching, marking the start of the Passover. Conveniently, "at the place where Jesus was crucified, there was a garden, and in the garden a new tomb, in which no one had ever been laid" (John 19:41)—a tomb cut into the rock of the cliff escarpment at the quarry's western edge. So, they laid him there, but they both knew—as did the women still watching from a discreet distance—that the job was hastily done. They had laid Jesus' corpse on a side-slab, a temporary resting place for preparing the body for its final burial in a shaft grave. That burial was sufficient—for now—but more would need to be done on Sunday morning. After rolling the stone across the entrance—to prevent disturbance by dogs and vultures—they spoke quickly to the women, agreeing on a plan of action, and then went their separate ways—grieving deeply at the end of their longest day.

Jesus at the Empty Tomb

SUNDAY *(early morning)*

ACT XI: The Encounter with the Risen One

Joseph, Nicodemus, and the women leave the tomb and return to their homes in Jerusalem—weighed down with grief. In other homes, children are excited as they prepare to celebrate their annual Passover meal and to enjoy the start of a week's holiday but not so for Jesus' followers. The next thirty-six hours would be the lowest point in their lives: a Sabbath of enforced rest, spent in sorrow and sadness. The women could quietly prepare for that moment early the next morning when, at last, they could set out back to the tomb, but for now all they could do was grieve.

Exterior photo of the Garden Tomb

What happened next would transform their grief into joy and their abject despondency into shouts of praise. For all four Gospels (together with the rest of the New Testament) insist that death was not the end for Jesus. The cruel drama of Friday's Crucifixion was followed by a dramatic demonstration of divine power on the Sunday. As Luke would summarize the matter in his sequel to his Gospel, "After his suffering, he [Jesus] presented himself to them and gave many convincing proofs that he was alive. He appeared to them over a period of forty days and spoke about the kingdom of God" (Acts 1:3). Simon Peter, writing towards the end of his life, would start his letter by speaking brazenly about a "living hope" that believers might know—all based on "the resurrection of Jesus Christ from the dead" (1 Peter 1:3).

Countless books have been written and endless debates engaged as to whether this, the consistent witness of the New Testament writers, can be taken seriously or not. Surely they could not be making such an absurd claim? Perhaps they were speaking figuratively about Jesus' teaching and influence carrying on after his death—a "resurrection" of a spiritual kind? Are not these claims for a physical resurrection of Jesus' body just the

Ancient first-century burial cave with large rolling stone at its entrance

result of their living in a prescientific era and playing fast and loose with the facts of real history?

There are many things that could be said in response to such understandable questions, but for now we simply clarify but one crucial point: the word for *resurrection*, which the New Testament writers used in their claims for Jesus, was a Greek compound word (*ana-stasis*), which was brutally physical and referred in its two constituent parts to a "standing-up" (*stasis-ana*). Jesus' body was once horizontal, they claimed, but then became vertical. His corpse "stood up!" Everyone in the ancient world agreed with the obvious truth stated in one of the plays of the great Greek playwright Aeschylus that "when the dust has soaked up a man's blood, once he is dead, there is no resurrection ('*anastasis*')." Some in the Pharisaic sect of Judaism ventured to believe that at the very end of time there might be an "*anastasis*" for the righteous, but no one was expecting this to happen in the normal course of history. It had never happened before, and no one was expecting it to happen now. Yet, according to the Gospel writers, it did!

We close by going back to the story which the Gospels tell about that Sunday morning. Imagine what you might have seen if you'd been standing on the walls of Jerusalem around six o'clock.

A few women, huddled close together, are silently and unobtrusively making their way out through the Gennath Gate long before most people are awake. You wonder: where exactly are they heading at this early hour? What are they carrying wrapped up in their cloaks?

Now it's the first week in April. The rainy season is past. It's promising to be a bright, warm day with the skies crystal clear. But right now, with the sun's rays not yet breaking over the crest of the Mount of Olives, it's still bitterly cold and the atmosphere decidedly damp.

The small expedition, evidently trying to be unnoticed, makes its way furtively into an area just outside the city walls that had been a disused quarry but which now had some vegetation and spring flowers sprouting up within it. Soon, however, the women disappear from your sight—obscured by a small outcrop of rock which stands up within the quarry, blocking your view.

Less than a minute later, you see two of then running back towards the city gate. They've evidently dropped whatever it was they'd been carrying and are running as fast as their legs can carry them. Minutes later you see the rest of the women coming back too. But these slightly older women are not running, but walking in a seemingly distraught manner—clasping hold of each other, as if they think any one of them might soon be about to faint.

Your interest is now fully engaged, and you stay standing on the walls—wondering what you might see next. Within five minutes, you see two young men running out from the city towards the quarry. The younger one steams ahead of the older one, who has a bigger frame and is struggling somewhat with the pace. Moments later, they too are walking back towards the city gate. The younger one is looking cheerful, gesticulating in an excited manner, but the older one stills looks heavy-hearted and perturbed.

You're about to go down to investigate this strange garden area for yourself when you see one of the younger women—one of the two you'd seen first—now going back out toward it. You decide to go down, walk out through the city gate, and follow her at discreet distance. A few moments later, conveniently hidden from her view by that outcrop of rock, you tilt your head to peer round the corner, and you see her pacing around in circles in front of a tomb cut into the quarry wall.

"They have taken away my Lord," you hear her screaming, "and I don't know where they have laid him!"

Just then a man comes into view, and she starts beseeching him: "Sir, if you have taken him away, tell me where you have laid him!" She is agitated and desperate, but suddenly she hears him speak a single word (her own name, "Mary!") and she turns and falls to her knees. "Master," she cries out in utter disbelief. With that one word, her body collapses forward—her hair and her hands now covering his feet. Evidently, she has found the person for whom she's been looking. But, he's clearly no longer in the tomb and, unless you're very much mistaken, he sure does not look dead. On the contrary, he looks very much alive!

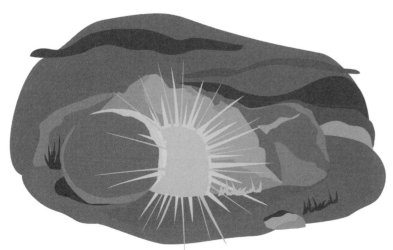

"He is not here. He is risen!"

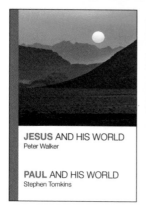

JESUS AND HIS WORLD
Peter Walker

PAUL AND HIS WORLD
Stephen Tomkins

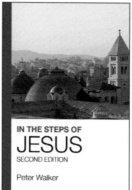

IN THE STEPS OF
JESUS
SECOND EDITION

Peter Walker

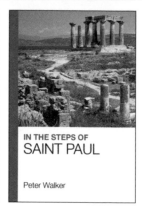

IN THE STEPS OF
SAINT PAUL

Peter Walker

For Further Reading

If you have enjoyed the Passion Play and would like to look more closely at the story of Jesus as described in the Bible, Dr Peter Walker has written some other books which you might find helpful:

Jesus and His World (Oxford: LionHudson, 2003; revised "scholar" edition, 2019). ISBN 978-1-91255-215-3.

- Your introduction to the historical Jesus, viewing his life and ministry against the background of his first-century Jewish world.

In the Steps of Jesus: An Illustrated Guide to the Places of the Gospels (Oxford: LionHudson 2007; revised "scholar" edition, 2018). ISBN 978-1-9125-5205-4.

- An overview of Jesus' life, taking you through each of the places he visited and giving you all the archaeological and historical information you need about those places before and since.

In the Steps of Saint Paul: An Illustrated Guide to Paul's Journeys (Oxford: LionHudson 2008; revised "scholar" edition, 2018). ISBN 978-1-91255-201-6.

- A similar overview of Paul's life, taking you through each of the places he visited—from Damascus to Rome.

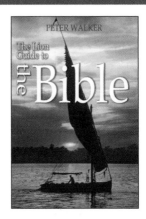 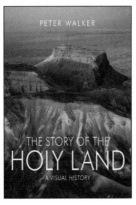 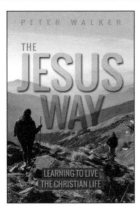

The Lion Guide to the Bible (Oxford: LionHudson, 2010). ISBN 978-0-74595-292-5.

*   A friendly "companion" to guide you through the whole Bible, giving you a brief summary of each of its 66 books, with helpful maps and diagrams of biblical history and geography.

The Story of the Holy Land: A Visual History (Oxford: LionHudson, 2013). ISBN 978-0-74598-053-9.

*   An overview of the history of the Holy Land, taking you on a journey from the days of Abraham to the present day, complemented by lavish photographs.

The Jesus Way: Learning to Live the Christian Life (Oxford: LionHudson; revised edition, 2020). ISBN 978-0-85721-960-2.

*   Based on two Bible stories (in Luke 24 and Acts 2), an introduction to Christian discipleship, giving twelve key steps for those wanting to be Jesus' followers today.

These books are available from www.lionhudson.com or your local Christian bookshop. For these books, as well as all the latest information about Peter's teaching and tours, please see Peter's website (walkwaybooks.com), where you can also obtain further copies of this book.

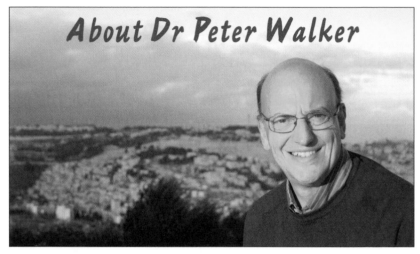

About Dr Peter Walker

Dr Peter Walker studied Classics and Early Church History at Cambridge University and has done extensive research at post-doctoral level on attitudes to Jerusalem in the time of both the Bible and the Early Church. For many years, he taught New Testament Studies at Wycliffe Hall within the University of Oxford and was for five years Professor of Biblical Studies at Trinity School for Ministry near Pittsburgh in the United States.

Dr Peter Walker has led guided tours to the lands of the Bible for over 30 years. He has authored a dozen books and written numerous articles on Jesus, the New Testament, and the Holy Land today. Peter is an ordained clergyman in the Church of England. He and his wife, Georgie, now live back in the United Kingdom and have two married children.

Notes